POSITIVE PERSONALITY PROFILES

POSITIVE PERSONALITY PROFILES

"D-I-S-C-OVER"
PERSONALITY INSIGHTS
to understand yourself... and
others!

TO: DONNA
God bless you!
Robert A Rohm

by
ROBERT A. ROHM, Ph.D.

PERSONALITY
INSIGHTS
INCORPORATED

ATLANTA, GEORGIA

Published by Personality Insights, Inc.
Post Office Box 28592
Atlanta, Georgia 30358-0592

ISBN 0-9641080-0-3

First Edition, September 1992
Second Edition, February 1993
Third Edition, March 1994
Fourth Edition, August 1994
Fifth Edition, September 1995
Sixth Edition, March 1996
Seventh Edition, May 1996
Eighth Edition, August 1997
Ninth Edition, July 1998
Tenth Edition, September 1999

Printed in the United States of America

Table of Contents

Dedication

In November, 1991, I spoke to over 7,000 school teachers at the Association of Christian Schools International Convention, in Anaheim, California. Teachers were asked to fill out comment cards, and after they were reviewed by the ACSI staff, they were passed on to me. As I looked through them, I came across a very touching and moving remark:

"Thank you for telling me God gave me my own unique personality. I have been a Christian for 23 years, involved with Navigators, Campus Crusade, and a counseling ministry. Fifteen years ago, someone told me I needed to let God change my personality. I tried to let Him do it with all my heart. Nothing seemed to work. I argued internally that He made me a certain way. Why would he change me? I tried everything. Now, today, the information you shared has brought everything into focus. It is like a 100-pound weight has been lifted. I am still struggling to gain emotional control. Thank you, thank you, thank you!"

In view of the fact that I have spent over 20 years as an educator, and because I personally believe school teachers are some of the most influential people on the face of the earth, I dedicate this book to ACSI school teachers, my co-laborers who are trying to help young people learn and grow. I trust the information in this book will give you clear insights regarding yourselves, your children, and your students, in order to help you be more productive on a daily basis. God bless you!

Foreword

I am happy to write these few words of introduction for my friend of many years, Dr. Robert Rohm. *Positive Personality Profiles* is a powerful book. Robert is one of the clearest communicators I have ever heard, and the truths he communicates in these pages can change your life.

I can say that because communication has been my life. I believe it is the key to happy, healthy relationships as well as success in the financial world.

Coming from a "high 'D / I' profile" myself, I believe in and appreciate the principles found in this book. We apply this system in my own company and have profited immensely from it. You are in for a real treat!

Zig Ziglar

Zig Ziglar Corporation
Carrollton, Texas

Acknowledgments

First, I want to thank my faithful secretary, Nancy Enis, for typing, re-typing, re-re-typing, etc., etc., this entire manuscript. She is not only a good typist — her editorial comments and recommendations have been so very helpful.

Next, I thank Bryan Pillsbury for his computer expertise in our first edition. He has already entered the 21st Century mentally. I'm still trying to learn how to turn a computer on! How did we exist before computers and people like Bryan to help us?

I thank my colleague, Dr. Mels Carbonell, for teaching me about personality types in a way I could understand. He first introduced this material to me while I was in graduate school in Dallas, Texas. Although I have studied and learned much over the years, Mels showed me the value of this material and how it could benefit other people. The "Practical Applications" come most from his wisdom, his insights, and his pen.

Finally, I thank God for the unique family He gave me. It helps in understanding personality types when you have at least one of each personality type living with you. That way the material is not only fresh — it is real! It comes from the test tube and laboratory of life. I am a believer in this information because *I have seen its results* on a daily basis. I am one happy camper!

This may sound selfish, but if no one ever gets anything out of this material but me, it would be well worth it because of what it has meant in my own life and relationships. I only wish that I could have learned it sooner. It should be required starting at about age 10. It could produce a lifetime of helpful results. Thank you Donna, Rachael, Esther, Elizabeth, and Susanna for being my best examples and teachers!

Preface

In the early 1950s, every Tuesday night, a faithful, single lady drove 50 miles from Atlanta to Griffin, Georgia, to teach a flannelgraph Bible story to a group of unruly boys. I know they were unruly because I was one of them! She taught us a wonderful lesson every week. Because she was such a good teacher and so well prepared, we didn't have time to misbehave as much as we would have liked. We tried — but she kept on loving us and teaching us. To this day, I still sense her love for our little class. Now, we who were in that class are all grown. Nearly everyone who attended those classes is now in full-time Christian work. Love is a powerful force.

As I have grown, and hopefully matured over the years, I have observed that one quality is sadly missing from most churches: love. Jesus said, "By this all men will know you are my disciples, if you love one another" (John 13:35). Of all things to say, why did He say the one characterizing quality of true disciples would be *love* for one another? It would have made more sense to have said, "By this all men will know you are my disciples if you... build a large church building," or "...give a lot of money," or "have a lot of people on your membership roll," or "have great results in your evangelism and missions programs." There is nothing wrong with any of these things. However, none is the mark of a true disciple as Jesus defined one.

So, over the years, I have kept asking myself these questions: "Why is it that people in churches, who know so many Bible stories and have even memorized verses, cannot get along with each other? Why can't people in families cooperate with one another?" Along the way, I was shocked to learn the number one reason missionaries leave the mission field is because they cannot get along with other missionaries. Why...? Why...?

Then, through a series of events you will read about in this book, my eyes began to open — I saw it clearly! The reason people do not love each other is because *they do not understand each other!* How can you love someone you do not understand, someone who is totally different from you, with a distinct way of thinking and acting that is foreign to the way you think and act?

The answer to that question revolutionized my entire life. It has affected my every relationship. It restructured the way I see my wife. It redesigned the way I parent my four daughters. It rebuilt my ability to love and accept other people. Now I realize why Jesus said, "By this all men will know you are my disciples, if you love one another." He was smart — He knew exactly what He was saying. I have finally discovered the key that unlocks that mystery — it is contained in this book.

As you read this material, I hope I will make it clear how you, too, can truly learn to love other people and appreciate the unique way God has made each of us. Love is a powerful force!

One Final Word...

I will be using masculine pronouns throughout this book. My only reason is to make reading easier and less wordy. For the sake of space and reading speed, I will use one gender, rather than "he or she," "him or her," "his or her," etc. I am no male chauvinist — God cured me of those tendencies long ago. I live with five women: a wife and four daughters. I am a minority in a sorority. I live in a girls' dorm... sometimes a girl's locker room! My greatest fear in life is walking into the bathroom one night, and getting tangled up and dying from pantyhose strangulation! I also fear the hole in the ozone layer will be traced to the use of aerosol sprays coming from the bathrooms in my house! I do have a male dog!

Introduction:

The Model of Human Behavior

Human behavior is both a science and an art.

It is a *science* in the sense that it's observable and repeatable. It's empirical in nature. We can objectively study it and obtain specific data from it. Research has enabled us to notice that most people have predictable patterns of behavior.

It is an *art* in the sense that we can experience it, modify it, and enjoy it. We can *feel* our behavior and adjust it according to our circumstances and environment. Your personality is somewhat like your "natural state." Someone has said it is the way we are when operating on "automatic pilot."

When I refer to personality as being our nature, I mean it is the way we operate when we're most relaxed with ourselves. It's the way we're "wired." You would not expect a newborn tiger to act the same as a newborn deer. They have different "natures" (or temperaments). If you were to approach them, you would do so differently because they *are* in fact different! You would adapt and adjust to the circumstances their natures demand.

Looking further into the animal world, we find enlightening illustrations. (As we develop our study, seeing things in the extreme may help us to see them more clearly in the narrow.) So, the nature of a lion is very destructive. He's called the "King of Beasts." As a way of life, he kills and destroys. A lion would not make a very good household pet! On the other hand, a French poodle certainly wouldn't be viewed as a ferocious beast, but simply as a cute little dog to have around the house. We can see in the animal world that creatures have different "temperaments," "personalities," or "make-ups." They are designed to be a certain way at birth. Unfortunately, they do not possess the ability to "think things through" and act appropriately. They simply *react* to most of their circumstances and situations.

Anyone knows that you should approach certain animals differently and treat them differently, based upon *what you know about them*. The same is true with people. In order to have the best relationship possible with other people, you need to treat them a certain way, based on how they are "wired."

As humans, we have a mind — and we should be able to think more clearly than an animal. We may feel we should be "ferocious" in one situation; funny in another; quiet in another; even pensive in still another set of circumstances. One of these moods may feel most comfortable to us, but as we learn about different personality styles, we will gain ability to adapt ourselves — depending on the circumstances — to act appropriately. We may have the temperament of a wild lion or a cute puppy, but by the act of our mind and will, we can adjust ourselves to our situations and use correct behavior.

It is important at the very outset of our study together that we remember we're not trying to "find" a certain style of behavior or a special personality type. Rather, we are looking at differences in behavior. The point of our study will not be "good or bad," or "right or wrong." Our forum will be the *differences* in personality styles. After all, if I understand you and you understand me, doesn't it make sense that we will have a better relationship? Let's get started!

Chapter One:
The "Four Temperament" Model of Human Behavior

There are four basic personality "types," also known as "temperaments." The complex ways in which these traits blend make up each person's distinct personality style. To help you understand why you feel, think and act as you do, let us take a graphic overview of the "Four Temperament Model of Human Behavior."

The four types are like four pieces of a pie. These parts are interrelated in fascinating ways, combining in multiple patterns, so that no one's unique personality is totally defined or influenced by only one set of characteristics. In fact, it is the limitless combinations of these elements that account for the great diversity of personalities.

OUTGOING – RESERVED

Outgoing

Reserved

To understand the concept, let's begin by cutting our pie diagram in half, representing two simple classifications of human personality: the top half represents people who are **"outgoing"** or fast-paced, while the bottom half represents people who are more **"reserved"** or slower-paced. Outgoing people are more active and optimistic. Reserved people are more passive and tend to be a little more cautious (some would say *realistic!*) One disposition is not *better* than the other — they are simply *different,* and both are important.

Outgoing (Fast-paced)

There are several ways we could describe **outgoing, fast-paced** people. They are primarily characterized by the word "Go!" It is in their blood. They love to be on the move. If a friend calls and asks, "Would you like to *go* to...", they have heard all they need to hear — the answer is "Yes!" It doesn't matter if the outing is all that great, or not. These individuals will make it great. Rather than look for excitement, they create it. They take their "party" with them wherever they go.

They are fast-paced and energetic. They like to do everything in a hurry. Be careful when you eat a meal with these individuals. You will still be on your salad while they are looking at the dessert menu!

They are optimistic and positive, looking for the diamond in every lump of coal, the gold in every clump of dirt. Generally, they like to win, and oftentimes win with flair. Outward appearance is very important to them — often, more important than inward qualities.

They involve themselves in projects, civic clubs, PTA and church groups, all kinds of organizations, and usually hold a leadership position. They like being in charge of things, not because they like to work, but because they like to tell others what to do! This doesn't mean they are lazy — far from it. They do not know when to quit. Their motto might be: "If a little is good, then more must be better!" Unfortunately, that is not always true.

This type of individual does not lack much in self-confidence. His eyes are often bigger than his stomach. He sometimes bites off more than he can chew, but to him, that's okay. He will "hustle" and make up the difference. If you have seen the bumper sticker that says, "Be a Leader... Be a Follower... or Get Out of My Way!", you understand it was written for the outgoing, fast-paced personality type. (And it was probably written *by* one, too!)

Reserved (Slower-paced)

There are also several ways to view those whose individual personality style is a little more **reserved,** or **slower-paced**. These individuals tend to be your "Steady Eddies." They may be the proverbial "tortoise" who is left in the dust by the outgoing, fast-paced "rabbit" type, but as in the classic fable, they usually end up crossing the finish line ahead of those who started the race with greater flourish. They have lots of patience and stamina to get the job done. This poem typifies these individuals:

> Life's battles don't always go
> To the stronger or bigger man,
> Sooner or later the one who wins,
> Is the one who says, "I can!"

Reserved types are cautious and reluctant to get involved in too many activities. "All that glitters is not gold!" can often be heard coming from their lips. They would rather look into a situation for a longer period time than immediately jumping in and going off "half-cocked."

The old proverb, "A wise man looks well into a situation, but the simple fail to do so and get punished," describes their philosophy of life. The carpenter's saying originated with them: "Measure twice... and cut once!"

Reserved, or slower-paced, individuals sometimes are accused of being too critical or "picky." But this quality actually helps them to see the reality of a situation very quickly. They tend to look below the surface to what is actually under the "top layer." To these people, quality is important. More than looking good, they want to know if it really is good. They have an excellent discerning spirit.

Although they tend to operate behind the scenes, they get the job done and make sure everything is handled correctly. They do not like surface relationships, and often find it difficult to have a lot of friends. They would rather have one or two really close friends than have a crowd around them. They are often "homebodies," and do not feel an urge to be "on-the-go" all the time. They prefer not to be surprised by unfamiliar situations. Indiana Jones is not their hero nor role model!

Summary Thought

Outgoing, fast-paced people can balance their own personality style by learning how to be more steady and cautious. **Reserved, slower-paced** types can balance their own personality style by learning how to be more demanding and inspiring.

TASK-ORIENTED — PEOPLE-ORIENTED

We can also cut our pie diagram in half the other way, representing two more distinct classifications of human personality: some people are more **"task-oriented,"** while others are more **"people-oriented."**

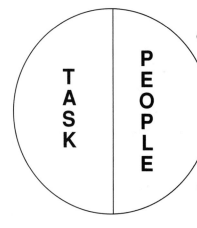

Task-oriented individuals enjoy doing "things," like making plans or working on projects. People-oriented individuals like to interact with other people, how much they care. They are more concerned with the way people feel than simply accomplishing a task.

Task (High-tech)

The task-oriented, high-tech personality finds great pleasure in a job well done. To these people, nothing is better than a fine-tuned, well-oiled, peak-performing machine. They are into form and function. Their favorite day of the month is when their bank statement arrives in the mail. They think, "Great — I will have this thing balanced in a matter of minutes." And they usually do! If you need someone to be in charge of organizing a program with lots of details (like a school graduation), put a task-oriented individual in charge. They will make sure every detail is covered — twice! They are excellent planners who can see the *end* of a project from the beginning.

However, a word of caution is in order: Oftentimes, they can be so concerned with getting the job done that they can easily hurt someone's feelings. They do not mean to, but because the overall task is more important to them than the feelings of any one individual, "the show must go on!" Again, they do not mean to hurt anyone, but being task-oriented, they have a difficult time experiencing empathy for the feelings of others if it conflicts with accomplishing the task at hand.

These people are great at working on projects. They can really get into the process of seeing a job take shape, then watching it get accomplished. For example, if you watch them rake their yard on a Saturday morning, you will observe that they first come out with a rake, look the yard over (like a field marshal preparing his battle plans), and then having done so, take the task in hand. They rake one section of the yard at a time, completing the job as efficiently as possible.

Pity their poor neighbor out for a nice, comfortable Saturday morning stroll. When he speaks to his friend who is raking the yard, the task-oriented individual usually replies with a quick, "Hi!", never missing a stroke. He simply keeps raking as he secretly thinks, "Oh no, I hope my neighbor doesn't stop and talk my ears off. I'm not out here to visit. I'm here to rake!" Should the unsuspecting neighbor continue to talk, he may find himself interrupted by the one with the rake: "Excuse me... I'll be right back." Do you know where he is going? Yes — into the garage to get another rake for his friend! He thinks to himself, "Two can rake better than one, and if he wants to talk, I'm willing to listen, as long as I can get this job (task) completed." That is just the way he's wired.

People (High-touch)

Contrast this scenario with the high-touch, people-oriented individual. They are interested in relationships with other people. Their motto seems to be: "I don't care how much you know. I want to know how much you care!"

These people are into caring and sharing. They like a dynamic group where there is a lot of talking, feeling, empathy, openness, and sharing of one's heart.

Because these people are more sensitive and are concerned with the feelings of other people, they handle the Saturday morning yard work very *uniquely,* with an entirely *different* motivation. Rather than being driven to get the *task* done, they are more concerned with what the neighbors might think if the yard looks bad (people-oriented). In other words, they feel compelled to rake the yard out of a need to be liked. They have a strong desire to be aware of the needs and desires of other *people.*

If someone walks by and begins to talk to them while they are raking, the first thing that goes through their mind is, "Oh good! A friend has stopped to see me!" If the neighbor stays any length of time at all, it will not be long before an invitation is extended. "Why don't we go into the house and have a cup of coffee and visit? I didn't want to rake the yard now, anyway!" Such is the nature of a people-oriented personality... Life is for the main purpose of developing friendships with many, many people.

Summary Thought

Task-oriented people can balance their own personality style by learning how to be more empathetic with others. **People-oriented** types can balance their own personality style by learning how to plan their work, then work their plan.

PUT IT ALL TOGETHER

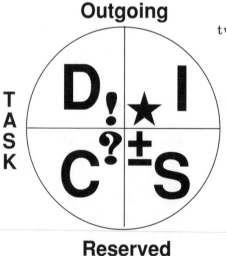

When we combine the two "cuts" of our pie diagram, we can see four temperament types:

Notice that we have added four letters to the diagram: D–I–S–C. In clockwise order, our "D" individual falls into both categories of the outgoing *and* the **task-oriented**. The "I" is both outgoing *and* **people-oriented**. The "S" is **reserved** *and* is also **people-oriented**. And the "C" personality is found to be both **reserved** *and* **task-oriented**.

Note: It's extremely important that you *"see"* the model at this point. Understanding it is vital, since this model will be used throughout the book to explain how the temperaments act, react, and interact with each other.

Review

"D" Type:
The "D" is in the top half of the diagram (the "outgoing" section), and it is on the *left* side (the "task-oriented" section). Thus, the "D" type personality is outgoing and task-oriented.

"I" Type:
The "I" is in the top half of the diagram (the "outgoing" section), and it is on the *right* side (the "people-oriented" section). Thus, the "I" type personality is outgoing and people-oriented.

Both "D's" and "I's" are active and outgoing, but each has a different motivation. The "D", being task-oriented, has a strong desire to get a certain job accomplished, while the "I" type, being people-oriented, wants to look good and desires status and prestige.

"S" Type:
The "S" is in the bottom half of the diagram (the "reserved" section), and it is on the *right* side (the "people-oriented" section). Thus, the "S" type personality is reserved and people-oriented.

"C" Type:
The "C" is in the bottom half of the diagram (the "reserved"

section), and it is on the *left* side (the "task-oriented" section). Thus, the "C" type personality is reserved and task-oriented.

Both "S's" and "C's" are reserved, but each has a different motivation. The "S", being people-oriented, has a strong desire to please people, while the "C" type, being task-oriented, wants to focus on getting the job done.

Remember, one type isn't *better* than another. We are not looking for "right" or "wrong," "good" or "bad" behavior. We are considering the *differences* in personality styles.

WHAT DO THE LETTERS D–I–S–C MEAN?

The letters in the four quadrants are *very significant.* They are your "hooks" for remembering the model of human behavior. (By hooks we mean a way to "catch" your memory. If you put a hook on the wall, your hat can be hung in place. Without "hooks," memory is like Teflon — nothing sticks!)

Remember, as we look at these four parts of the pie together, we are able to visualize the "Four Temperament Model of Human Behavior." *Each of us is a unique blend of these four parts.*

"D" Type:
The letter "D" (outgoing and task-oriented) stands for the **Dominant, Driving, Demanding, Determined, Decisive Doer**. Notice that all these words start with the letter "D." More will be said about the "D" type personality in Chapter Two. But for now, the key concept to grasp is 1) Outgoing; 2) Task-Oriented; 3) Dominant (or other "D"-type descriptive word). A symbol has also been added to each quadrant. For the

"D" type, we see an exclamation point, because this typifies the "D" type's "make it happen now" attitude! (Three qualities and a symbol will characterize each personality type.)

"I" Type:

The letter "I" (outgoing and people-oriented) stands for **Inspirational, Influencing, Inducing, Impressive, Interactive, Interesting, Interested** in people. Notice that all these words start with the letter "I." More will be said about the "I" type personality in Chapter Three. For now, the key concept to grasp is 1) Outgoing; 2) People-Oriented; 3) Inspirational (or other "I"-type descriptive words). Our defining symbol is a star, because it typifies the "I" type's "make it fun" attitude, and a personality that tends to "perform" and become the center of everyone's attention.

"S" Type:

The letter "S" (reserved and people-oriented) stands for the **Supportive, Submissive, Stable, Steady, Sentimental, Shy, Status-quo, Specialist**. Notice that all these words start with the letter "S." More will be said about the "S" type personality in Chapter Four. For now, the key concept to grasp is 1) Reserved; 2) People-Oriented; 3) Supportive (or other "S"-type descriptive word). Our visual symbol is a plus and a minus sign, because "S" types can respond with either "more" or "less," depending upon their surrounding influences. They are very flexible and can go either way. ("It doesn't matter to me, whatever you want to do is fine with me.") This symbol typifies the "S" type's "I'll go along with you" attitude.

"C" Type:

The letter "C" (reserved and task-oriented) stands for **Cautious, Competent, Calculating, Concerned,**

Careful, Contemplative. Notice that all these words start with the letter "C." More will be said about the "C" type personality in Chapter Five. For now, the key concept to grasp is 1) Reserved; 2) Task-Oriented; 3) Cautious (or other "C"-type descriptive words). Our symbol is a question mark, because it typifies the "C" type's "does this make sense?" attitude and need for resolution.

THE TOTAL PICTURE

By now, you have probably thought, "I feel like I have some of all these traits. I have some D–I–S–C in me." Exactly! You are a unique blend of these four traits. Each of us is "wired" differently. Some traits are more dominant in us than others. Research shows that in about 80% of the general population, people have at least two areas that tend to dominate their personality style, while the other two areas are less dominant. (More will be said about this as we develop our study together.)

In other words, it is rare to find a person who is *solely* a "D," or an "I," or an "S," or a "C." Usually we are a *combination* of at least two of these traits. However, one of these traits may be so prevalent that it dominates a person's life. Other personality aspects will still be present, only to a much lesser degree of intensity.

Much more will be said about "behavior patterns" (or "classical patterns" or "blends") in later chapters. These interchangeable terms describe the way each person's blend of D–I–S–C makes up his or her own unique personality.

What do you call it?

By now you may be thinking, "I have heard some of this

personality stuff before... I just can't remember what it is called." That may be because the old Greek titles, used long ago, have no "hooks" to them.

Most people struggle with remembering these personality types, recognized and named by Hippocrates, the father of modern medicine. As early as 400 B.C., Hippocrates theorized that temperament types resulted from the four bodily fluids which are predominant in one's body: 1) yellow bile; 2) blood; 3) phlegm (pronounced *flem*); and 4) black bile. So, he derived his names of the four temperaments from the names of the four liquids he thought were their primary cause:

- Yellow bile > the active type > Choleric
- Blood > the lively type > Sanguine
- Phlegm > the slow type > Phlegmatic
- Black bile > the dark type > Melancholy

The words "choleric," "sanguine," "phlegmatic," and "melancholy" are not only difficult to pronounce (because they are not a part of our daily vocabulary), but also we have no frame of reference to help us in categorizing those terms.

Using the old Greek terms can be very confusing. For example, when I was on a radio talk show in New York City, the gentleman interviewing me asked me to explain the "collar-ic" personality (like a shirt collar?). My mind went totally blank — "What is he talking about?" I did not realize he had simply mispronounced "choleric." There were only two thoughts that came to my mind. First was "colicky," and I thought to myself, "Isn't that what small babies get when they have an upset stomach?" And the other word was "cholera" — and I knew that was a disease! Only a few seconds went by, but it seems like an eternity. Finally, I replied, "Oh, you're talking about the 'ko-LAIR-ick' personality type!", using the preferred pronunciation. He laughed and said, "Yeah, that's what I meant!"

My point here is that most people do not use the ancient Greek terms for the model of human behavior because they are hard to remember, have no applicatory "hook," and are very difficult to pronounce. For those who are familiar with the words, the "D–I–S–C" pattern follows in this order:

"D" or **dominant** type is equivalent to the old Greek **choleric** (ko-LAIR-ick) temperament;

"I" or **inspirational** type is the old Greek **sanguine** (SAN-gwin) temperament;

"S" or **supportive** type is the old Greek **phlegmatic** (fleg-MAT-ik) temperament;

"C" or **cautious**, **competent** type is the old Greek **melancholy** (MEL-en-kol-e) temperament.

Even though the idea that bodily fluids determine one's personality has been long since discarded, the fourfold classification of temperaments is still widely used. It was not until recent days that a modern classification of temperaments has been arranged. The D–I–S–C system is one of these methods. (Nine commonly-used classification models are reproduced in the Appendix for your reference.)

As we proceed, we will show how it is better to have the "hook" of D–I–S–C in one's mind, rather than using the old Greek titles, which most people do not relate to and find difficult to remember.

SUMMARY

By now, you have a clear picture of this Model of Human Behavior in mind. You may need or want to review it several times, until you feel as if you "own" it. Again, it is the model we will use throughout the remainder of this book.

Review Questions: (Check the following page for answers.)

1. What two qualities characterize the "D" type personality?
2. Give one "D" word that characterizes the "D" type personality?
3. What is the characterizing symbol for the "D" type personality?
4. What two qualities characterize the "I" type personality?
5. Give one "I" word that characterizes the "I" type personality?
6. What is the characterizing symbol for the "I" type personality?
7. What two qualities characterize the "S" type personality?
8. Give one "S" word that characterizes the "S" type personality?
9. What is the characterizing symbol for the "S" type personality?
10. What two qualities characterize the "C" type personality?
11. Give one "C" word that characterizes the "C" type personality?
12. What is the characterizing symbol for the "C" type personality?

Answers:

1. Outgoing and Task-Oriented.
2. Dominant.
3. Exclamation point.
4. Outgoing and People-Oriented.
5. Inspirational.
6. Star.
7. Reserved and People-Oriented.
8. Supportive.
9. Plus and minus sign.
10. Reserved and Task-Oriented.
11. Cautious.
12. Question mark.

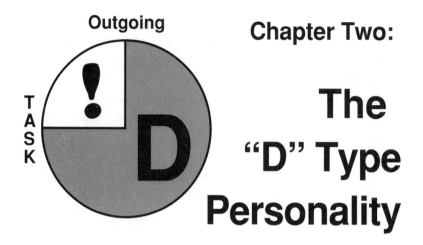

Outgoing

Chapter Two:

The "D" Type Personality

Our "D" type personality is both *active* and *task-oriented.* Keep a mental image where this type falls in our model of human behavior (unshaded area noted by the exclamation point).

"D's" are **drivers** and **doers**. They make the world go around. They are movers and shakers. They have things to do, places to go, people to see. You had better "fish or cut bait!" Do not look for too much sympathy from "D's." They don't express a lot of warmth or empathy. They'll be quick to tell you, "Quit sucking your thumb and get back to work!"

"D's" have a tendency to be **dynamic** leaders. They never say die. If at first you don't succeed, try, try again. The famous coach Bear Bryant was asked in the late 1960s, "Coach Bryant, you have won three national college football championships in this decade. What more could you want?" He replied, "I want to win it every year!"

"D" types have a flair for the **dramatic**. That helps them achieve the seemingly impossible. The late Pete Maravich, who played for L.S.U. in the late 60s still holds 32 college basketball records. Think about all the great college basketball players who have played since the days of "Pistol Pete." Before each game, coach Press Maravich, Pete's dad, would say to his son, "Pete, take people to a place they have never been before." And he would do it! What a dramatic place to go!

The "D" type is very **demanding**. They seldom take "no" for an answer. A "no" to them means "ask again later!" If you stick to your "no," they will be thinking of a way to go around you. They are not being rebellious — they just have so much **drive** and **determination** that they want to keep going. Frank L. Stanton wrote a poem that aptly described how these driving "D" types feel:

> If you strike a thorn on a rose,
> keep a'goin,
> If it hails or if it snows,
> keep a'goin,
> Ain't no use to sit and whine
> when the fish ain't on your line;
> Bait your hook and keep on tryin'
> Keep a'goin!

I was riding down the highway one day and a big truck passed me. On the back was a sign which read, "We are first... because we last!" I thought to myself, "A high 'D' must own that company!"

"D" types have a lot of nervous energy. Their minds are always going 100 miles a minute. They thrive on movement and involvement. They must have a mountain to climb, a project to work on, or a challenge to motivate them. Ten irons in the fire at once are not uncommon. They figure if five fail they are still several ahead of everyone else. Alexander the Great died at the age of 33, crying, "I have no more worlds to conquer!" Bear Bryant once said, "I would hate to give up coaching. I would be dead in six months." After retiring, he was dead in six weeks.

It doesn't take a rocket scientist to begin to see how the active, task-oriented "D" type personality would easily be the kind of person who would make an excellent **dictator**. They feel like they must be in charge. Although they have a natural tendency to be a "take charge" kind of person, that does not mean that they must *run over* everyone. There is a real tension between being a leader and being a servant. A leader must be able to take control of a situation and make quick, accurate decisions. That is the way you get to be a leader. Let's face it — a leader must lead! However, a leader must also be a servant.

Think of all of our elected officials, our medical personnel, school teachers, and clergy. They are all in the *serving* professions to help people. In reality, everyone is in a serving role to one degree or another. But those in serving roles with "D" type personalities will have a tendency to let their leadership ability *overpower* their serving ability. At any rate, both qualities are important, but must be kept under control. A "D" type who understands himself will be able to lead *or* serve, depending on the circumstance and situation.

The "D" type usually seems to be very **dogmatic**. They take a position quickly and stick to it — unless they see a better idea or plan — then they quickly change to the new method of operation. Those who work with them, especially under their authority, sometimes have a difficult time knowing what is going on in their minds. You see, "D's" interject change as a constant mode of operation. Because they are so "bottom line" oriented, it is easy for them to change virtually any situation in midstream. In a "D's" way of thinking, everyone should be like them and be flexible enough to adapt to any situation.

The "D" type can also appear to be **defiant**. They project the attitude, "It's my way or the highway!" They definitely do not like taking orders or being told what to do. Fortunately, this quality *rightly directed* helps them to stand alone and can cause them not to be interested in being like the rest of the crowd. "D" types usually will not be led astray by the "wrong crowd." They may be the *gang leader* in one of these "crowds," but not a follower. Defiance used correctly oftentimes can be one of their greatest assets.

Percentage of Population

Research seems to indicate that only about 10% of the general population has this type profile. (I have often thought that God was merciful to us by only giving us 10%!)

Biblical Example

The best Biblical example of a high "D" type personality would be the Apostle Paul. Before Paul became a Christian, he was a **dogmatic, domineering, driving, demanding doer**. After he became a Christian, he was a **dogmatic, domineering, driving, demanding doer**! His personality did not change; however, *who* was in control of Paul's life did change.

Before he became a follower of Christ, he was killing Christians (Acts 22:4, 20). Afterwards, he himself was willing to die for the cause of Christ (Acts 20:24). That's the way it works with a "D" type. They are able to swing from one extreme to the others without any problems. By the way, it is interesting to note that Paul focused on *control* and allowed *change* to come as a by-product. "Be *controlled* by the Holy Spirit. The fruit will *result* in love, joy, peace, patience, kindness, goodness, faithfulness, gentleness, self control" (Galatians 5:16–22).

It was understanding this scenario in Paul's life, perhaps more than any other, that opened my eyes to the truth concerning personality types. I could literally see the Apostle Paul's high "D" type personality on "both sides of the fence." Without the control of the Spirit, he was out to destroy people and churches. Under the control of the Spirit, he was able to help people, start new churches, and write most of the New Testament. What a contrast! Yet it was the same **dogmatic, domineering, driving, demanding** type personality that helped him move onward and upward in both causes.

Personal Illustration

When I first became interested in personality types, it was almost out of desperation. It seemed to me that my oldest daughter, Rachael, was getting more and more *out* of control. I once heard that Mark Twain said, "When a child is born, put him in a barrel. Leave a hole big enough for air and water. When he becomes a teenager, plug up the hole!" When Rachael turned 13, I started looking for a barrel. I found myself constantly asking, "What is the matter with my daughter? Why is she so stubborn and hardheaded? What happened to that sweet little girl who used to ride on my back?"

A friend of mine was visiting me and my family in our

home. I was going through graduate school at the time. He asked me if I had ever done a personality profile on Rachael. I said, "What is that?" He explained that a personality profile is an assessment from which a child chooses answers in order for you as a parent to understand how they are "wired" inside, how they are made. He showed me a child's personality profile and we let Rachael go through it and fill it in.

When my friend scored it, he looked at me and said, "Uh, oh." I said, "What??" He said, "Well, she's what you call a high 'D' type personality." "What's that?", I asked. He then began to explain to me the personality types *in a way I could relate to and understand.* I felt like scales were falling off my eyes and I could really see.

Basic Need

My friend told me, "Because you have a high 'D' type daughter, you need to parent her differently. High 'D's' must have *challenge* and *control.* These are their basic needs. When you say to her, 'Rachael, you need to go to bed by ten o'clock,' she hears something entirely different from what you said. Rather than hearing, 'You need to go to bed by ten o'clock,' she hears, 'Do you want to fight?'"

I thought to myself, "Wow, that must be right! She likes to fight about everything!" I had to learn to say the same thing in a different manner. So that night I thought I would try it. I said to Rachael, "Tonight you can go to bed whenever you would like. Ten o'clock is the limit, but you choose." She looked at me and said, "Okay!" And that night at ten o'clock, she went to bed... and I picked all my teeth up off the floor! I was amazed! I realized that it was the first time I had conscientiously tried to raise her according to her own particular "bent," rather than just force her to obey me. By the way, Proverbs 22:6 states, "Train up a child in the way he should go, and when he is old he will not turn from it." In the past I had completely misunderstood this verse. I thought it said, "Train up a child in the way *I want* him to go...." Rather it states, "Train up a child according to his own unique bent or personality...." Now for the first time I was realizing how to do that. (Note: For further study on Proverbs 22:6, please see *Appendix A* in the back of this book.)

I was sold. The more I began to study this material, the more I saw how practical and applicable it became. I began to parent Rachael, as well as all my children, differently (as will be explained throughout this book). I began finally to understand my wife for the first time — and we had been married for 15 years at the time! I can honestly say that every relationship I possessed began to be influenced by this newly-acquired information.

I had read about personality types years earlier and knew there was something to it. Unfortunately, I had not been taught in a way in which I could get a handle on it. Now, all the pieces were beginning to fall into place. It suddenly made sense. My background as an educator began to come into focus. I rearranged and clarified the concepts in order to communicate them to my own family as well as others.

Strengths

The "D" type personality, like all four type personalities, has its strengths and weaknesses. "Strengths" could be described as natural tendencies. A lot of these "D" type qualities were developed in life as they grew up. Their environment naturally attracted them to learn some traits while neglecting and ignoring others. For example, both a "D" and an "I" type might easily be drawn into a debate or speech class because they are both active and outgoing and they like to talk; therefore, skills along those lines might be developed.

The "D" type is strong-willed. Their tendency is to be both determined and independent. They do not need anyone telling them what to do! (So they think!) They are optimistic. They always feel the next plan or project will be "the big one!" They do not like to be around pessimistic people. It drives them crazy! I once heard a high "D" say, "Most people I know look like somebody just licked all the *red* off their candy!" Don't try to lick the red off their candy!

One night I drove over to pick Rachael up from her job. While she was finishing up I talked to the restaurant manager. I said to him, "How is Rachael doing here at work?" He looked around the room and whispered to me, "She's like nobody I have ever seen before. If someone is not doing what they are supposed to be doing, she will take their job away from them and do it herself. I think she could run the entire organization. She really does a good job. I'm just a little concerned she has her eye on my job!" I thought to myself, "Yep, that's my girl!"

Isn't it amazing… the very way God had made her human personality was the very thing I tried to change completely, all because it was different from mine.

When Rachael graduated from high school and moved away, our home instantly began to experience a greater degree of peace. Please do not misunderstand me — we love our daughter with all of our hearts; however, because "D's" thrive on conflict and are so "headstrong" and are willing to "go to the mat" over everything, it just makes life easier when there is not that constant conflict and struggle for power and control.

It is hard for those who have a high "D" profile to develop intimate relationships with other individuals. Sadly, they often go through life crushing other individuals, not knowing the damage they are doing. "D's" typically feel like everyone should be a "D" and should be a mover and shaker in life. It has been my experience that sooner or later, every high "D" will meet someone who is a higher "D" than they are, who will put them in their place.

This was graphically illustrated to me by a former college football teammate of mine, perhaps one of the finest running backs in the country. One time I asked Billy what went through his mind before a game. He told me that he knew there was at least one person on the opposing team who was better than he was and he would have to do everything in his power to overcome that. Instead of that realization making him lose control, he focused on staying under control. It simply made him a more able opponent. His ability to carry a football was not diminished in the least, but strengthened because he understood himself and his opponent. By the way, it should be noted that oftentimes, "D's" do look at other people who try to stop them in their efforts as *opponents*. "D's" will make dynamic leaders and cause a lot of good qualities to be developed in other people if they can just keep themselves under proper control.

"D" types are very practical. Sometimes their pragmatism gets them into trouble. Because they are so "bottom line" oriented, they tend to be blunt and to the point. However, their practical nature helps them to be very productive. They are not into *talking* about something; they are into *doing* something. As noted earlier, their motto easily could read, "Be a leader, be a follower, or get out of my way!" Over the gate leading to the practice field at the University of Alabama, Bear Bryant placed a small sign. It read: "Be Good or Be Gone!"

"D" types are decisive decision-makers. They may not always be right but they are always confident. If they turn out to be wrong, well it was a good learning experience. I have a good friend who is a high "D" type who lost an $80-million office complex due to the weak economy at the time. He *laughed* as he told me the story. He ended by saying, "Life is too short to worry about what went wrong. I will just keep trying, and sooner or later, things will turn around. I will get it back." And with that attitude, he probably will!

"D" types make great leaders. If they participate in football, they will usually play quarterback or middle linebacker. If they like baseball, they will be the pitcher or catcher — both giving signals telling each other what to do! Most of the great leaders in the world have this type personality. It is the kind of "stuff" from which great leaders are made. Let's face it, if you have "thin skin," get criticized often and cannot take it, you simply are not going to make it as a leader. When it gets too hot in the kitchen, you are going to get out! "D" types have the confidence it takes to "stick with the stuff!" They can make the hard decisions even in the face of difficult opposition.

"Somebody Said It Couldn't Be Done," by Edgar A. Guest, could be the life-poem of a "D" personality:

> Somebody said it couldn't be done
> But he, with a chuckle replied
> That maybe it couldn't, but he would be one
> Who wouldn't say so till he'd tried.

He waded right in with a trace of a grin
　　On his face; if he worried, he hid it.
He started to sing as he tackled the thing
　　That couldn't be done — and he did it.

Somebody said, "Oh, you'll never do that.
　　At least no one ever has done it."
But he took of his coat and he took off his hat;
　　And the first thing we knew, he'd begun it.

With a lift of the chin and a bit of a grin,
　　Without any doubtin' or "quit it,"
He started to sing as he tackled the thing
　　That couldn't be done — and he did it.

There are thousands to tell you it cannot be done;
　　There are thousands to prophesy failure;
There are thousands to point out to you, one by one,
　　The dangers that wait to assail you.

But just buckle in with a lift of your chin,
　　Take off you coat and go to it.
Starting to sing as you tackle the thing
　　That cannot be done — and you'll do it!

Weaknesses

　　It must be remembered that weaknesses are simply
strengths that are taken too far and thus become abuses. Most
of us operate on the basis of our strengths until we get in a
difficult situation. Then we are prone to get out of control, let
these "strengths" get the best of us and shift into our "over-
strengths" or weakness mode. (If you are *not* a "D" type, it might

be a good idea to remember when reading about these weaknesses not to feel too smug. Your chapter is coming!)

"D" types can be extremely angry. They tend to have a short fuse and a hot temper. They often can explode in anger over the least little thing. Remarkably, they get over it just as quickly. While others are reeling and rolling in the wake of their explosion, the "D" type has forgotten all about it. They forgive and forget faster than any of the other personality types. To them, it's history — forget it and move on.

"D" types can be cruel and sarcastic. They can pound you into the ground by their words and actions. I have worked for five different pastors over the last 20 years. Four were "D" type personalities! Under the control of God they had great influence for good over the lives of many, many people. Out of the control of God, they could be as cold as ice.

My father was in a bank one day transacting some business. As he got ready to leave, he noticed that the teller had given him two $20 bills too much in change. My father went back to the lady and said politely, "I believe you made a mistake." The woman looked at my father, snapped at him and said, "I don't make mistakes!" My father, realizing he was dealing with a "hothead," politely replied, "That's fine. But this afternoon when you come up $40 short, I have it!", and then turned to walk out. Suddenly, the bank teller changed her tune and said, "Oh, sir, I am sorry. Maybe I did make a mistake."

You see, when a high "D" realizes that what's wrong is going to cost them something, they are more prone to change their mind. Their tendency can be to run over people at times, but they certainly do not want anyone to run over them.

Because "D" types are strong-willed, which is good, they can also be domineering at times. If they do not get their way, they start looking for an alternative method to get their way. If they think they cannot get their way, they may leave. I believe people misread Ross Perot when he got out of the early 1992 presidential contest. He was not accustomed to "nobody reporters" talking to him like he was on trial. He got interested in the race because he felt he could lead America economically. But excuses aside, the nonsense associated with politics overwhelmed him.

"D" types can be inconsiderate at times. Looking out for Number One (themselves) comes naturally to them. It is not that they are selfish. It is just that they figure if they are well taken care of they will be in a better position to help others, also.

They often appear to be proud, displaying an air of superiority. Again, they do not mean to communicate superiority, but rather *confidence*. After all, who wants to be around someone who exudes a poor or bad self-image?

Recently, I was watching a television series about powerful individuals. It showed how they followed a four-step progression in their lives. I could not help but think how a lot of "D" personalities could fall into this trap. The first step was *alone* — they like to do things by themselves and have no one tell them what to do. The second step was *arrogant* — they felt like they knew more than other people and were smarter and maybe even better than other people. The third step was *adventurous* — in that they wanted to have a life filled with action-packed adventure; the more, the better. The last step was *adultery* — when they felt like they wanted to conquer another person. These four steps can be avoided if a person recognizes his strengths and weaknesses and puts them under the control of the Holy Spirit.

"D's" sometimes can be crafty, having a "hidden agenda." They know what they want to do, but do not want you to find out about it. They are excellent at behind-the-scenes manipulation. Usually when a "D" type goes into an important board meeting, he had done his homework. He has already had several "pre-meetings" with individuals and knows how the votes will be cast and what the outcome will be before anyone else. He does not feel very good about leaving things up to chance.

"D" types can be very self-sufficient, relying on their natural abilities and talents to get them through difficult situations. They are so much more productive when they learn to go outside of themselves for additional help or input. People working under their authority often fear going to them with new ideas. "D" types can cut you off before you even get halfway into your thoughts. A smart "D" learns to listen and has an "open spirit" toward people. He thereby benefits greatly.

One day, my high "D" daughter was making some toast. She completely burned six pieces into coal. The smoke filled the house, and I was really upset. I threw the smoking toast out the back door into our yard. Since she was 12 years old at the time, I said, "How can you be 12 years old and not mature enough to cook six pieces of toast?" I was disgusted at her lack of maturity. I said, "I'll cook the toast." So I put six more pieces of bread in the oven.

While they were browning, I got a phone call from an out-of-town friend, to whom I had not spoken in a long time. I got enthralled in our conversation, until... I smelled something burning — again. I opened the oven and saw six more charred pieces of toast. Soon, there were twelve pieces of burned toast in the back yard! Rachael looked at me and said, "I can't believe you are 35 years old and can't cook six pieces of toast!" She was right, and we got a laugh out of it. "D's" hate to be wrong. High "I's" (like myself) hate to look bad. Between the two of us, we turned it into a pretty funny story.

Finally, the "D" type has the tendency to be very unemotional or unfeeling. He seldom cries or displays tender affection. It just is not in his makeup. His way of showing love can be very strong if you understand his mind. He likes to buy or produce "things" to show his affections.

"D's" Make Good:

"D" types make excellent producers, leaders and builders in any field. They make great coaches and military officers. They make good policemen and political leaders. They make good preachers, teachers, and corporate presidents. They make good criminals! Their profession or role in life may vary, but their personality will not. It will be churning inside them to go and grow, to move and shake, to advance to bigger and better horizons. As previously noted, "D" types make the world go around. They are never satisfied with status quo. They are constantly looking for new and better ideas and ways of doing things. We owe the "D" types a lot of gratitude!

Review

"D's" love *conflict*. It makes their blood flow faster. They *feel* comfortable and at home in a war zone. Therefore, they have special needs. How they feel may seem totally foreign to you, but I can assure you how *you* feel is totally foreign to *them!* They must have a *challenge.* A big challenge motivates them. The bigger the challenge, the more they like it! But beware — when their mind is no longer on the project, they are gone! They are off in a new direction, looking for new projects to attack — uh, I mean attract!

For example, if they are in real estate, they find a piece of property, have it surveyed, begin cutting roads and hauling out trees, see the foundation of the first home poured, and by that time, they lose interest in the project. They see that it is well enough along for them to begin a new project! It takes a good "C" type personality to complete the loose ends of a "D." (We will learn about the "C" type later in this book.)

"D" types also need *choices.* They do not like to be poured into the same mold as everyone else. They are constantly looking at bigger and better alternatives. If you work for a "D" type and really want to shine, give them two or three choices regarding a situation you have been assigned, and then, make your recommendations. Finally, end by saying, "We can combine some of these choices, or we can look at some other options you have in mind — w*e can do whatever you want to* do.*" You* just rang their bell!

Finally, "D's" need control. They must feel like they are giving direction to a project or they will quickly lose interest. If they cannot be in charge, they will start looking for greener pastures. It is not that they are selfish or self-centered. They just have so much drive and determination that they feel useless unless they have some "hands-on" project they can control.

"D" type personalities need an environment where there will be some *conflict, challenge, choice,* and *control.* They work best under these conditions. An environment including these qualities will help them "rise to the occasion." Some readers will think, "I would hate to work in that type of environment." Exactly! Remember, there are two keys we are learning to use: One, how to better understand *yourself.* And two, how to better understand *others.* After all, if I understand you and you understand me, doesn't it stand to reason that we will be in a position to have a better relationship?

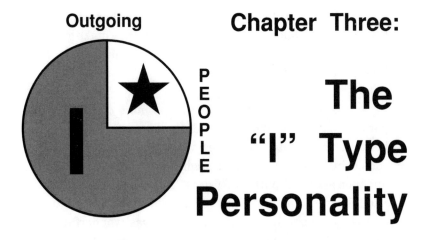

Outgoing

Chapter Three:

The "I" Type Personality

Our "I" type personality is both *active* and *people-oriented*. This illustration shows where these people fall in our model of human behavior (unshaded area noted by the star).

"I's" are **inspirational**. When you are with them, you feel great. To them all of life is a good time. They help you have a "mountain top" experience every time you are together. After all, the mountain top is where they love to live!

I heard a joke that there is a new therapy group designed for people who love to talk. And, of course, wherever you find a high "I," you will find someone who loves talking. The new therapy group is called "On, and on, and on, and on, and on!"

High "I" types are **influencing**. They can sell snowballs to snowmen. They make everything sound great. It is good to be optimistic, but often they influence you by making things sound better than they actually are! High "I's" can influence you with their "charming" ways. Because they are good talkers, they can make you believe almost anything. If they are honest, they can become great leaders and producers. If not, they make great con artists. They love to "wheel and deal." They make great "front line" people for any organization.

The high "I" quality is the predominate trait in my own personality profile. When I was dating my wife, I usually gave her three cards with her choice for the date of the night. It went something like this: Card #1 might have read, "Chinese food, and then play putt-putt golf." Card #2 might have read, "Seafood, and then go to a movie." Card #3 might have read, "Italian food, and then ice-skating." She thought it was wonderful that I would put such time, thought and preparation into our dates. After we were married she asked me one night, "Where are my three cards? I want to choose what we do on our date tonight." I then realized the deceitfulness of dating! High "I's" tend to want to have a lot of fun, and they can win just about anyone to their way of thinking. But be careful — after they win you over, the fun may seem to disappear!

"I's" are **inducing**; that is, they make things happen. They are cause agents. They are stimulators. They do not feel good unless something is happening. Calmness is not a part of their makeup. Whenever a group of people gets together, the high "I's" are the last to go to bed at night — and the last to get up in the morning. They stay up late because they do not want to miss anything, or because they are involved in some activity. (Unfortunately, it is usually a time waster to most people.) They like to sleep late because they figure there is not *that* much going on early in the morning for them to miss, anyway!

"I's" are **impressive**. They overwhelm you. As soon as they walk into a room, the entire atmosphere changes. Suddenly everything begins to "lighten up" (one of their favorite expressions). They believe life is too short to be miserable. They figure (as the old saying goes…), "If you can't be with the one you love, love the one you're with!" One of the reasons high "I's" make such good speakers, actors, salesmen, comedians, etc., is because all the world, to them, is a *stage* — and they are the main attraction! The show must go on!

A high "I" teacher usually wins the "Teacher of the Year" award because they are so much fun, make learning enjoyable, and may meet with more receptive learners. Their students usually enjoy being around them and hearing their "war stories." ("I's" won't admit it, but they never even have lesson plans. They usually "shoot from the hip!") They can inspire students, causing them to want to better develop themselves, their futures and careers. In retrospect, students may look back and see that they actually did not learn much information from that teacher. What actually happened was that they had a lot of fun and felt good about the experience of being in that teacher's class.

High "I's" are **interesting**. They know so many people. Usually they know a lot of important people. People are their life. The more, the merrier. They do not have to worry about going to a party — they take their own party with them wherever they go! They love to tell their stories, laugh, imitate other people, get you to laugh, and on and on. When they leave a room, you can suddenly feel the temperature drop. It begins to get colder because the "on fire" high "I" stepped out.

Many times, a high "I" will try to "one-up you!" In other words, no matter what you do, they can top it. Years ago, a conversation between two small children was overheard. One of the children was a little girl named Leigh Caldwell. Leigh is grown now and is a beautiful Christian wife and mother. As a little child with a bubbly high "I" personality, Leigh could "one-up" anybody. One day she was talking to one of her friends and said, "I can *swim*." Her friend said, "I can swim in the *deep* end." Leigh replied, "I can *jump* off the diving board." Her friend said, "I can *dive* off the diving board." Leigh escalated, "I can do a *flip* off the diving board." Her friend said, "I can do a flip off the *high* dive." So, Leigh said, "I can *water ski*." Her friend said, "I can water ski *on one ski*." At this point, Leigh was getting frustrated, because her friend was able to outdo everything she could do. Finally, after a few seconds of silence, Leigh looked at her friend and said, "I drowned before!" Her friend grew strangely quiet. She could not top that!

High "I's" are **impressionable**. That is, they are easily influenced. Although they are outgoing in many respects, they are also followers. They see what the latest fads and trends are, then go after them. They have such a strong desire for people to like them that they will do just about anything to please other people. Many times, they will be trend-setters themselves. They dress, behave, and function basically to call attention to themselves in one way or another.

When I was in high school, I had a coach who was a great encouragement to me. In looking back, I realize he had a real high "I" profile. Every day at practice, he made statements that gave me a great deal of encouragement. One day he told me if I were to stand on one goal line, and he were to get a rabbit and put it beside me, and let me and the rabbit race to the other end of the field, that the rabbit wouldn't have a chance! That made me feel so good inside and caused me to want to please him. On another occasion, he told me that Raymond Berry, the former great end of the Baltimore Colts, had just retired. He told me the Colts would probably draft me right out of high school to take his place. Again, his confidence in me caused me to want to fulfill his expectations. When we show high expectations in individuals, many times they will tend to fulfill those expectations.

Jim Sunburg, former catcher for the Texas Rangers and the Kansas City Royals, tells the following story:
I was visiting a prison one day, sharing a word of encouragement with the inmates. I told them when I was a boy, my father and I would play catch in the afternoon. One day, I threw the ball over his head and thought I was in trouble. But my dad said, "Son, anybody who can throw a ball that far is going to play in the big leagues one day." Another time, my father pitched the ball to me and I swung as hard as I could, but missed. My father looked at me and said, "Son, anybody who can swing a bat that hard is going to play in the big leagues one day. And another time, I hit the ball over the fence, through the neighbor's plate glass window. My dad said, "Son, anybody who can hit a ball like that is going to play in the big leagues one day." When I grew up, there was nothing left for me to do but play in the big leagues!

Jim continued, "After I finished speaking, a man came up to me who had chains around his ankles. He said, 'Mr. Sunburg, I had a dad sort of like yours. He told me I was no good and that I would never amount to anything, and one day I would end up in prison. I fulfilled his dreams for me, too.'" How important it is that we share words of encouragement and build confidence in those around us, especially our youth.

High "I's" like to be **important**. They hate little jobs or small tasks. They like to start at the top. They care more about a title and status than they do raw power. If a school teacher tells little "Sparky" to be good and he will get a *red star* next to his name, he is really pleased and thinks, "Oh boy!" (Tell high "D's" the same thing and they will think, "Keep your dumb star and let *me* be the teacher!")

"I's" are dreamers and schemers. They always are thinking about, wishing for, or letting their minds wander off to exciting adventures. They just know the "big event" of their life is around the next corner. If they harnessed all their thoughts, organized them, and put them into practical steps of action, there would be no stopping them. Unfortunately, most high "I's" are severely out of touch with their own feelings and with reality. They must remember — "all that glitters is not gold!"

The same feelings that make high "I's" desire to be important can lead them to great misery. The Reverend Jimmy Swaggart, by his own admission, was most of the time preaching to himself. He has stated that he faced severe problems with morals all his life, but had no one to turn to. Sadly, the same strong emotional desires that helped him preach to thousands of followers led him down the wrong path when he thought no one was watching. His public disgrace hurt many. Again, high "I's," more than any other type, face this roller coaster experience.

A lot of high "I's" are athletes. They love the glory of the athletic arena. Usually, they are wide receivers. They do not want to hit anyone, nor do they want to get hit. They like being clean-looking *before* and *after* the game. (My good friend and former All-Pro receiver Billy "White Shoes" Johnson is a prime example. He told me he played to have fun and look good — he never wanted to *hit* anybody!) They just want to shine — in the end zone. They are good competitors, but for their own reasons. Coaches who understand high "I" athletes know they can get twice as much from them with *praise*. They do not like to be "put down." If you "fuss" at them, they will usually quit trying. They feel, "You don't like me, so why should I try?" When you encourage them, they think you believe in them and their abilities. That is when they will "kill themselves" for you, in order to show you just how right you were about them!

"I's" are **interchangeable**. They are like chameleons — they can change "colors" very quickly to take on characteristics of their environment. They can be one way on Sunday (in church) and another way on Monday (at work). They have no problems with inconsistency. They figure everyone is **inconsistent**, so they just don't worry about it very much. If they fail to understand the implications of their personality traits, their lives will be one long roller coaster ride of highs and lows. They live day by day like a tumbleweed, blown along by whatever surroundings in which they find themselves. Ironically, no other personality type is able to set the tone or direction for activities as much as the high "I." When they face the truth that they may lose a few friends or be made fun of, and are still determined to do right, then they become **inspirational** leaders.

Perhaps the most colorful high "I" I have ever met was Mel Livingston, a friend I played football with in college. Mel was a person who actually *did* everything most people just *talked* about doing. In 1968, Mel decided to go to the Olympic games in Mexico. When he said, "I'm going to the Olympics," most people simply laughed, but those of us who really knew him knew that he probably would go. If you ever have opportunity to see highlights from those games, there is a group of people running along the track in front of those who carry flags from different nations. Look carefully, and you will see one blond-haired fellow with a big smile, waving at the camera — that's Mel Livingston! I have never met anyone who was as "gutsy" as Mel!

After that, Mel went to Auburn University to try out for a football scholarship and made the team during Spring training. The coaches later found out that he was not even enrolled at the school, and therefore, they could not give him a scholarship. An Auburn coach found him working in a gas station in West Point, Georgia. He told Mel, "Son, we have had plenty to quit, but we have never had one to sneak in!"

Again, Mel did the same thing at the University of Southern California. I remember the day Coach John McKay called our junior college coach and asked if he could get some grades on Mel Livingston. He said he was playing in the first-string backfield with O. J. Simpson, but had not enrolled in school. Those of us who knew Mel simply thought, "That's typical!" He had a lot of ability, but most of the time, unfortunately, it was unharnessed. The last word I heard about Mel was that he was some kind of physician in Arizona. I don't know if that is true or not. If it is true, I would almost bet he somehow did it without going to medical school!

High "I's" are **interested** in people. That is what makes them tick! They are concerned about what everyone thinks of them. They evaluate all projects by the level of interest shown by other people. They like to travel or go places in groups. Some people are happy just to have one close friend, but not high "I's." They love people and activity. They are interested in what everyone is doing.

I recently counseled a family with a very active teenage son. The parents could not understand why the son always wanted to be "on the go" with his friends. He could not understand why they always wanted him to stay home and read. They concluded that there was "just something wrong" with him. So, I gave all three of them (mom, dad and son) personality profile assessments. Both parents had a high "C" profile (more said about that it Chapter 5), but their son had a really high "I" profile. When I began explaining high "I's" to them, you should have seen the look on their son's face. His expression seemed to say, "Finally... somebody really understands me!" I explained to him how he needed to discipline himself or his unlimited potential would eventually "fizzle." A lot of "going and doing" can be great if coupled with maturity and self-discipline. I also explained to the parents how they needed to lighten up and learn to have some fun. They all left my office on better terms and closer as a family, because all three understood each other better.

I remember when I was growing up, telling my mother she had to let me do various activities because *everyone else* was getting to. She would often look at me and ask, "If everyone jumped into a fire, would you?" Although I never answered her, I did think to myself, "Well, if everyone else did, I guess I would, too!" High "I's" are not real logical! (Maybe a good "I" word would be **illogical**.)

High "I's" are not primarily interested in getting a job done — their primary interest is in how everyone gets along with each other during the job. Relationships are paramount, and those who get their feelings hurt should be loved... especially if "those" are them!

Percentage of Population

Research seems to indicate that about 25–30% of the general population has this type behavior as their primary driving force. That is a large percentage of the population. However, it is certainly in harmony with the number of comedians, actors, public speakers, and entertainers in our midst!

Biblical Example

The best Biblical example we could cite would be the Apostle Peter. He was so **impetuous**! He was the disciple who always spoke before he thought (open mouth — insert foot!). It is very interesting to read the story in Matthew 16:13–17. Jesus asked the disciples, "Whom do men say that I am?" After they "beat around the bush," Peter spoke up: "You are the Messiah!" Jesus commended him on the wisdom he had displayed and told him God was at work in his life. However, within minutes, Jesus told the disciples that he would soon face desertion and death (Matthew 16:21–23). And Peter rebuked Jesus, telling him it would never happen. Jesus, in turn, rebuked Peter, and called him *Satan!*

I began to wonder about that. How could Peter be so "in touch" one minute and so "out of touch" the next? Then I remembered the key issue: control! It all depends on whether you are under control or out of control. When you are under God's control, you have great value to God and other people. When you are out of control, you are of little use to God, other people, or even to yourself! Peter indeed learned his lesson — the hard way.

However, just because you have failed in a situation does not mean you are a failure as a person. No failure need be final. After the resurrection of Christ, God needed someone to stand up and proclaim the good news. In Acts 2, on the day of Pentecost, over 5,000 people were gathered together. Who do you think God called on to stand up in front of all those people and speak? Right — the Apostle Peter! He did a great job. He was right at home speaking to the multitudes by teaching and preaching. He was under God's control and brought great good into the lives of many, many people.

It is interesting to note that Peter wrote only two very short New Testament books. High "I's" struggle with writing. They have neither the patience nor the inclination to write. They dream about it and talk about it — they just don't do it. Usually, your "D's" and "C's" do all the writing because they are *task* oriented. The hardest part of graduate school for me was writing my doctoral dissertation. I had to discipline myself to do a little each day. Otherwise, I never would have finished it. It just gets to be too boring and laborious — no excitement. This may be normal, but it doesn't have to continue as the *norm* for a high "I."

Personal Illustration

Two of my daughters have high "I" type profiles, Esther (daughter #2) and Susanna (daughter #4). High "I's" like to have a lot of fun. As I have said, they don't ever have to go to a party — they take it with them everywhere they go! My second-born, Esther, "smarted off" to my wife, her mother, one day and I had to discipline her. My discipline, or training, of her differs from my discipline of Rachael (high "D," remember?). Esther loves to talk, so I said, "Okay, you smarted off to your mother. You know you cannot do that. Now you have phone restriction for three days." To tell high "I's" they cannot talk kills them. It is the worst discipline they can face. After only one day of not being able to talk on the telephone, she came to me and asked, "Daddy, could you just spank me?" She said, "I'd rather go ahead and get it over with. I have to talk on the phone!" I knew I had found the correct discipline for her.

I mentioned I have had to discipline (or train) each daughter differently. If you tell high "D's" they are on phone restriction, they will just think to themselves, "I don't need your phone. I'll buy my own phone one day, and then you won't tell me what to do. I'll have money one day and you will come to me needing a loan — and I will get you a loan... at prime plus two!" Can you see how we must raise, train, teach, and discipline each child differently?

Recently, my high "I" daughter Esther was having a hard time in her most difficult class of the day — study hall! High "I's" never like to sit still for an hour and study. It is possible for them to discipline themselves to study, but only if they do it in short time increments, and they need to be alone... not in a crowd. Some of the older students who had privileges were allowed to leave campus and go to a local restaurant for a few minutes to get a Coke. She called me, almost on a daily basis, to ask permission to leave as well. Her excuse to me was, "I'm only missing study hall." I was able to sit down with her and explain that I knew exactly how she felt. I told her I knew she didn't want to take the time to sit quietly in study hall for an hour at school while her friends were all out having fun.

I reminded her that her personality said, "Go and do!", but the responsibility factor where she was in life meant that she had to "sit and stay" in her study hall class every day. After I reminded her that her tendency was not to use her time wisely, she was able to "harness" herself, understand herself better, and work with herself. That is the bottom line of all this information.

We should each recognize our own, individual personality traits and work in harmony *with* ourselves, and not *against* ourselves. If we can learn to be a friend to ourselves, rather than our own worst enemy, we will all enjoy a more productive life.

My all-time favorite boxing champion was Joe Frazier. I once read an exciting article about him in *The Reader's Digest.* When Joe was training for his heavyweight fight with Muhammad Ali, he got up and ran five miles at four-thirty every morning. Joe said that many times, after he had run four-and-a-half miles, he could hear a little voice inside saying, "Why don't you quit? No one is looking. No one will know." Joe said he just kept running as he thought to himself, "Brother, *I* am the *last* person I want to fool!" I have never forgotten that story. If high "I's" are not careful, they may go through life fooling a lot of people, but none more than themselves!

Susanna, our fourth-born, high "I" daughter, is just a lot of fun. She went to spend a weekend with my mother, who is her grandmother. My mother tells me they were checking out of a dime store when Susanna spotted a wrist watch. "Please buy me this watch — I need this watch — I don't have a watch, Grandmama — will you please buy me a watch — please, please, please!!!??" My mother said, "Susanna, they are just junk! It's only a $2.00 watch, it won't work; it is just a piece of junk."

Susanna replied, "Please, Grandmama, if you really love me, you'll buy me the watch!" Well, you know that all Grandmamas are "suckers." My mother said, "Okay, Susanna, I'll buy you the watch." The next morning, Susanna was winding the watch, and as she wound it, it broke — you know: boingngngng! Pieces flew everywhere. My mother said she thought it would be a great opportunity to teach Susanna a lesson. So she said, "See,

Susanna, you should have listened to me when I told you not to get that watch, because it was just a piece of junk. If you had listened to me this never would have happened."

Susanna looked at my mother and said, "I should have listened to you?!? I *know* I should have listened to you. I'm just a little kid. But *you* listened to me. That's why we have this problem!" My mother told me, "I was so confused, I ended up apologizing to her! I didn't know what was going on!" High "I's" can turn things around on you so quickly that you don't realize what is happening. One of their mottos is, "I may not get *all* the credit, but I sure don't want *any* of the blame!"

By the way, after you grasp these personality insights, you will be better equipped to talk to your own children and students on a deeper level. They will be amazed when you tell them how they are feeling inside. And when you are accurate in your explanation, it will really get their attention. Then they will feel that you really do understand them and what they are going through. You have learned to see life through their glasses!

Basic Need

The most important quality you can ever offer a high "I" is *recognition*. Give them a little praise and attention, and they will follow you anywhere! "I's" are fearful they might lose their friends or their popularity. Consequently, they are susceptible to temptation. As I once heard someone say, "I can handle anything but temptation!" High "I's" need to be part of a group. They need to have close friends with whom they can be accountable. If you ever need their attention, just call their name out loud several times — it is the sweetest sound their ears can hear!

Strengths

High "I's" are very friendly. They seem to talk to or wave to everyone they see. They know no strangers. After you have been with them five minutes, you feel like you have known them all your life. They have few enemies because they are "people pleasers," wanting everyone to like them. Will Rogers once said, "I never met a man I didn't like." That is a typical high "I" statement.

High "I's" are compassionate. They tend to act before they think. They sometimes are willing to give you the shirt off their back, only to discover it is cold outside. A lot of their actions are motivated by "Do unto others as you would have them do unto you." (They are also very interested in your "doing" unto them — i.e., they figure if they are nice to you, then you *should* in return be nice to them!) They have *big hearts* because they like people so much. Unfortunately, they sometimes lack a *big head* and are easily taken advantage of.

High "I's" are carefree. They sometimes are guilty of living by the seat of their pants. They appear to be unstable at times, simply because they have a lot of restless energy. I once saw a book entitled, *Why Do I Feel Guilty When I Relax?* I thought to myself, "That must have been written by a high 'I'." Although it is good to have a lighthearted spirit about life, it does not always produce good results. My good friend Zig Ziglar says, "If you're hard on yourself, life will be easy on you; if you're easy on yourself, life will be hard on you!" High "I's" could learn a lot by focusing on this truth. (By the way, High "I's" like to mention the names of their important friends! It helps with their own **identity**!)

High "I's" can sometimes be overbearing, because they are

so talkative. They prefer noise to silence most of the time. "I's" seem to know a little bit about everything... or at least, they make you think they do, giving you their opinion or point of view on any topic. They usually are the first to speak up on a crowded elevator. Watch out if a high "I" approaches you as you are both checking out at the supermarket. They can and will talk to you about anything: receipts, food you've bought, your children, family vacation plans, and on and on. You will wonder, "Do I *know* you?"

High "I's" are very outgoing and enthusiastic. They are excited about — well, just about everything! They love get-togethers with their families and friends. Any reason will do — New Year's, Valentines, Easter, Memorial Day, Fourth of July, Labor Day, Thanksgiving, Christmas, birthdays, anniversaries — you name it, and they will be there! Think of just about any exciting television commercial you have seen. It usually features a high "I" doing all the talking. They are selling cars, promoting their law firms, bragging about their wrestling skills, showing off how much weight they have lost, and on and on the list goes. They are good up in front of people. To them, all the world is a stage and they are the main attraction! One of their favorite all-time thoughts can be summed up in the song, "There's No Business Like Show Business!"

High "I's" are warm and personable. They are the kind of people you want for friends. They are very transparent. When you are having a difficult day, they will be the first to try to cheer you up. They'll tell you all about something they went through and how well everything worked out. Pretty soon, you will begin to feel better. They have a way of looking at the bright side of life. As stated earlier, however, "I's" can also have mood swings in their emotions. If they are having a bad day, go out of your way to show them a little attention.

It won't take long before they begin to "bounce back."

In general, high "I" types have learned the secret of attracting others to themselves. When I was a little boy, my father took me to the zoo. On the way, we stopped at a Howard Johnson's Restaurant for lunch. As we were leaving, my father put about half a dozen sugar cubes in his pocket. When I asked him what he was doing, he said, "You'll see." When we got to Atlanta's Grant Park Zoo, we walked all around, looking at the animals. Finally, we came to the elephants. People were holding out their hands with peanuts in them. The elephants extended their long trunks and took the peanuts out of their hands. As my father put the sugar cubes in his hand, he whispered, "Watch this!" Suddenly, elephant trunks started moving our way — if we had not been protected by a barrier, they would have trampled us to death! We were the center of attention. Everyone wanted to know what we were using to attract the elephants. My dad told them... just as we ran out. As we were going home that afternoon, he said to me, "Never forget what you saw today. Always remember in life you can be a lot more productive with *sugar* than you can be with *peanuts!*" High "I's" understand that truth.

Weaknesses

As pointed out under the "D" category, weaknesses are simply strengths taken to an abuse. When we get under pressure or out of control, we often go into "overdrive." We begin to function by our natural inclinations, only more so. Remember, our strengths *carry* us — our weaknesses should *concern* us.

The high "I's" can be very weak-willed, pressured into doing things they should not do. Because the high "I" wants to be liked, he allows himself to be **illogical** at times. He tends to see the best in others; therefore, he expects others to do the same. When he suddenly finds himself "behind the eight ball," he quickly unravels. His morals, truthfulness, ethics and integrity all can suffer. If a high "I" understands himself, he can avoid being weak-willed through the power of the Holy Spirit and the discipline of self-talk: "I know I want these people to like me, but what they are asking of me is illegal (or immoral); therefore, I cannot do it. I may lose some friends, and that will be painful, but at least I can keep my integrity!"

High "I's" often appear to be unstable and undisciplined. They are very **impulsive** in their behavior patterns. Because they are so carefree, they sometimes fail to see the advantages of self-discipline. As mentioned earlier, the high "I," perhaps more than any other personality style, has unlimited potential — but sadly, often produces little more than a life of unfulfilled, broken dreams. If the high "I" charts a course of action, plans steps of accomplishment along the way, and is accountable to other people, there is no limit to future successes.

"I's" are restless. They find it hard to stay on track and complete a project. Their "direction finder" seems to be lost! Whatever career path they choose, they will be dissatisfied. They enjoy change too much! When they leave the doctor's office they think, "I would have liked being a doctor." When they leave church they think, "I would have enjoyed being a preacher." When they go to a ball game they think, "I would have been a great athlete." The grass is always greener somewhere else. They may go through several changes, looking for that perfect job or ideal environment. What they fail to realize is that "wherever you go… there you are!" If they recognize this weakness and face it for what it is (namely, a high "I" weakness), they will be able to do something about it and deal with it. There is nothing wrong with a career change, and certainly there is nothing wrong with wanting to better yourself. However, when all you do is jump from one job to the next, looking for peace and happiness, you seldom find it. I heard someone say, "You can never *find* happiness. Happiness finds *you!* It comes as a by-product of a disciplined life!" I have come to believe that statement is very accurate and true.

When my wife and I were first married, I was constantly involved in things that included a crowd. I would usually invite one or two of my friends (sometimes even more) home for dinner. I looked at our house as if it had become a mini-restaurant. My wife enjoyed having a lot of company, although in hindsight I will admit that I overdid it. Not meaning to, I communicated to her that I always wanted more people around than just her. I had to get this under control and realize that sometimes it is important *not* to be "the life of the party," and to save some time for solitude and aloneness as a couple. Again, it was not anything toward her; it was just me out of control!

"I's" tend to be loud. They have trouble listening, but no trouble talking. They are able to drown out others so everyone can hear what they are saying. Pretty soon, they have most of the attention as each group, one by one, turns its attention from its own conversations, to listen to the exciting exploits of Mister "I." He has two speeds: fast and full blast! Turn your "listener" up, or you will miss something.

One of the high "I's" greatest weaknesses is his undependable nature. At times he can appear to be very **inconsistent**. Again, this is because his eyes are often bigger than his stomach. He wants people to like him so much that he struggles over disappointing anyone. He often finds himself with calendar conflicts. He says "yes" before checking prior commitments. An excellent statement for a high "I" to learn is: "I'd rather 'let you know' than 'let you down.' Let me check my calendar and I'll get back to you." High "I's" tend to bite off more than they can chew, then hustle to make up the difference. Remember, again, this weakness is nothing more than the strength of being outgoing and enthusiastic, taken to abuse. Mister "I" is always on the move, excited about every opportunity that comes along. However, when he has gotten involved over his head, he then starts backtracking, feeling frantic about his circumstances, and starts to reveal his undependable nature. By the way, never tell a high "I" a secret. They love to hear secrets, but cannot keep them to themselves. They always tell someone... in "strict confidence!"

Another weakness the high "I" faces is having an egocentric lifestyle. In other words, it is easy for everything to revolve around *self*. When making plans, high "I's" will usually look at things from their own point of view first. If *they* like it, they are sure everyone else will, too!

"I's" have a natural tendency to exaggerate a lot. The last book was the best book they ever read; the last movie was the best movie they ever saw; the last good restaurant had the best meal they ever ate, and of course, every song is their favorite song! The reason is because they are so emotionally wired. It is not uncommon to see an "I" express emotions openly. Tears are his friend. (They can even be used to his advantage!) "I's" are very expressive and use adjectives abundantly — they help paint the picture of the story they are telling. The miller in the fairy tale story of "Rumplestiltskin" told the king his daughter could spin straw into gold. He got her into an extremely difficult situation! The miller was definitely a high "I"!

One time, when my daughter, Esther, was very small, she and my wife were at a shopping mall. Esther hated to go shopping. She felt like she was being tortured going from store to store. She kept misbehaving. Finally, my wife looked at her and said, "Esther, if you don't behave, I am never bringing you shopping again." Esther thought for a minute, then looked at my wife and said, "Do you mean if I'll be real bad, I won't have to come back again?!" She was definitely thinking about her own well-being!

One other weakness the high "I" possesses is being fearful. Although on the outside he appears to enjoy risks, on the inside he is scared. What if things don't turn out like he said? He will be laughed at and mocked — nothing could be worse. Although he expresses full knowledge of what is going on in his environment, he sometimes has more confidence than ability!

"I's" Make Good:

High "I" personality types make good actors. They love the stage. They also can act offstage! As children, high "I's" can laugh one minute and cry the next. As teenagers, they can convince you of almost anything as they act the part of a martyr, a hero, or whatever their circumstances demand.

They also make great sales people. They maneuver around your mental roadblocks faster than you can say, "I'll buy it!" The only problem with high "I" sales people is that they sometimes talk too much and forget to ask for the order. It is important to them that they are persuasive in a way that is "winsome" to the customer. That way, even if they don't make the sale, they still win, because at least you walk away liking them. High "I" employees can benefit by having short attainable goals and a productivity-measuring standard. Otherwise, they may visit a customer, make a great impression, enjoy the process, but fail to be productive in making the "bottom line" sale.

Finally, "I's" make great speakers. They are good one-on-one, but even better in front of a crowd. They are not reluctant to speak, whether prepared or not. Their view is: "Open your mouth — *something* will come out!" They make great radio announcers, motivational speakers, evangelists, auctioneers, or con artists. (It just depends on self-control and integrity.) They excel in any vocation where talking is the main focus.

Review:

High "I" types are the life of the party, the class clown, the best storytellers, and a lot of fun. Give them a little *recognition* and they will love you forever. They make the world a more colorful place.

High "I's" sometimes feel like life is a fast roller coaster ride. Their emotions are constantly moving. They can be higher than a kite or lower than a skunk!

They will do just about whatever it takes to get attention. If they get "on track" and find an avenue whereby they can use their talents, they will usually go far in life. If not, their lives will be a long chain of broken dreams. "To whom much is given, much shall be required" (Luke 12:48). High "I's" have been given a lot of gifts and abilities; therefore, much is expected and required from them. If they have self-control, their potential is limitless. They can be a source of great blessing to many people.

Chapter Four:

P
E
O
P
L
E

Reserved

The "S" Type Personality

Our "S" type personality is both *reserved* and *people-oriented*. Keep a mental image where this type falls in our model of human behavior (unshaded area noted by the plus and minus signs).

"S" types are **steady** and **stable**. They like doing one thing at a time. Routine may be boring to some people, but not to them. It gives a great deal of security knowing things are constant and in order. The old saying, "a place for everything, and everything in its place" was first spoken by an "S" type personality.

These individuals both communicate and desire a great deal of **security**. They *communicate* it in the sense that they want you to know they will always be there for you. They *desire* it in the sense that they want to know you will always be there for them! They can keep secrets to themselves without ever telling anyone.

I have a friend who has a high "S" profile. Although he is

a precious person, he is a real people-pleaser. You must admire the desire of a high "S" to please. They are willing to go the second, third, and even fourth mile. After he completed his first Doctor of Philosophy degree, my friend started worrying that he had not done enough to make his family proud of him. So, he went back to an even bigger, more well-known school and completed a second Ph.D. degree! Fortunately, his efforts have paid off and the experience didn't cost him his sanity. He now realizes he probably achieved his goals for all the wrong reasons, because he had lost touch with why he was doing what he was doing.

He came from an alcoholic family that wouldn't — and probably couldn't — give him the appreciation his personality type needs. He would stay at school, working long hours, to avoid conflicts at home. *"S's" hate conflict.* He stayed at school even over the holidays, except for Christmas Eve and Christmas day, to avoid family strife. The day after Christmas, he returned to school to continue his studies or to work out in the athletic facility.

He once told me, humorously enough, that the strangest thing he ever discovered in college was the debate team. "Why in the world would anyone want to argue for competition? That is a real mystery to me. I avoid arguing like the plague, and here is a group of people trying to be on a team to do it!" I can still see him shaking his head, laughing and saying, "I couldn't believe it!" If you are an "S" type personality, you understand perfectly what he meant.

Perhaps the best "S" word concept that helps us focus on this personality is the **supportive** (or the **servant**) type. "S" types make up a great percentage of our serving professions. They are great helpers. The hardest word for an "S" type to say is the word "no." They are "yes" people. They look for ways to cooperate and help. They want you to feel loved and supported. A lot of people don't like the word "servant." They think it sounds medieval and belittling. Actually, we are all servants in varying degrees. Life's highest calling is to be a servant. Even Jesus called himself a servant (Mark 10:45). When we seek to help those we serve to the best of our ability, we make them look good, and in turn, we profit from these actions.

I have a friend who is a vice president at Merrill Lynch. He was in a situation where several brokers were meeting with a man who had just sold his business for $40 million. Each was presenting a proposal to get this wealthy man's business. My friend, Bob, reasoned to himself, "How can I best serve this man?" He did a lot of research and found out that $40 million would draw $6,000 per day in interest (after taxes) in a certain account. When Bob made his presentation, he pointed out this fact — also, that he had done all the preparations necessary to enable the man to receive $6,000 *beginning that day* if he chose to invest with Bob's company. After all of the brokers had made their proposals, the man chose my friend Bob as the one to represent him, basing his decision on the fact that Bob was looking out for his best interests beginning that very day. Of course, I have related this story because Bob has a high "S" profile, and it is natural for him to look for his client's best interest. He has a servant's heart.

Regardless of your personality style, you can develop this habit of looking for the best ways to serve others. It is easier for high "S" or high "I" types because they are people-oriented, but anyone can cultivate this mind-set if they will work at it.

"S" types are **sweet**. I have never met an "S" type I didn't like. They are just so special. They are not pushy or bossy. You just like being around them — they make you feel right at home. Your "comfort zone" finds delight when you are in their presence. They always take a back seat, and give others the opportunity to be first in line. While there is just something about human nature that makes us all dislike a "know-it-all" bossy person, the "S" type comes across as just the opposite. So, everyone responds positively and likes them. The funny thing about this is that "S's" don't do anything deliberately in order to make you like them. That's just the way they are — they would be that way even if no one else was around. They are sweet people!

The "S" type is also **submissive**. They take orders very well, perhaps too well. I have often thought that a lot of "S" type young people are really good kids, but have gotten themselves into trouble with drugs, immorality, etc., simply because they have such a hard time saying "no." They like to please. They try to do what you want them to do. Is it any wonder the "Just Say No!" anti-drug campaign does not work for some students?

Another characteristic of the "S" type is **shyness**. They usually prefer to sit in the back of a room so no one will notice them. They hardly ever raise their hands to be called on. They prefer to go unnoticed. It is not that they don't like people — far from it. They love people. They just don't want to be pushy. They love to have fun and enjoy a lot of excitement — just as long as it doesn't center around them.

I was speaking at a convention for school administrators in Atlanta. Afterwards, a man came and stood around with several other people. After everyone had spoken to me and the crowd had disbursed, he still stood there, alone. He looked at me and said, "Hi, I'm a high 'S' and I wanted to wait until everyone was finished so I could talk to you." I thought to myself, "That figures." A high "S" is polite and has manners. This man had waited for several people to talk to me. Although he had been there ahead of many of them, he didn't want to be rude to anyone.

He said, "I just wanted to come tell you how much this information has helped me. Several years ago, my wife and I got married and we understood absolutely nothing about personalities. Our marriage was a disaster. We fought constantly. Both of us were miserable. We later discovered why. We found out that my wife was a high 'D' and I was a high 'S.' That created some real problems in our relationship. She wanted me to lead, but I was more willing for her to lead. I felt like she tried to run over me all the time, and I never wanted to challenge her. The more she wanted to lead, the more I wanted to retreat. But every time I tried to lead I felt like she resisted me, so I easily gave up. After a while, our marriage ended in divorce. We just didn't understand personalities at the time."

He continued his story: "After two years, we got back together to go to a marriage counselor. Neither of us had remarried, and we wanted our original marriage to work if at all possible. The counselor gave us the Personality Profile Assessment and explained to us why we thought and felt the way we did. He gave us information and guidance on how to adjust our personalities in order to have a good working relationship. After we understood ourselves, we began to work together. We remarried each other and we are happier now than ever before. I just wanted to come by and tell you that."

I reached out and gave him a hug. Almost overwhelmed, I said, "You 'S's' have the best stories. You just won't tell anyone!" He was a real blessing, and his story illustrates just how important it is in a marriage relationship to understand yourself *and* your mate.

"S" types like **status quo** or **sameness**. As mentioned elsewhere, the reason for this is because they enjoy situations in which they find stability. One "S" word they don't like is "surprise!" They are more comfortable with the known and expected than with the unknown and surprising. If things stay the same, day-in and day-out, they feel comfortable because they know what to expect. They usually drive to work the same way, eat in the same restaurants, order the same food, go to the movie they have already seen twice, and visit the same vacation spots every year. This would be boring to some, but to an "S" type, it brings less *stress* (another "S" word they don't like!).

The "S" type is very **sentimental**. They know what they like. They have favorite movies, memories and moods. When a special occasion arises, they usually travel "down Memory Lane." They revisit the past often. It bothers them when places from their childhood change. They like things to remain as they always have been. They save all their old yearbooks, love notes, poems, and other memorabilia. Hopefully, they have saved their baseball cards!

Finally, the "S" type can often (and unfortunately) be a real **sucker**. This is certainly not because they are dumb. It has nothing to do with their *head,* but it has everything to do with their *heart*. They tend to think with their hearts. They often get talked into doing things they don't want to do — into buying things they don't need — and into going places they don't want to go. They do all this to please people. They can become great "enablers." (This term refers to someone in an unhealthy environment who is not actually the sick one, such as an alcoholic, but is the one who helps or enables the situation, so the sick one can keep his sickness going. Enablers "cover" for their alcoholic friend, rather than "raising their 'D'" and saying, "Look, you need help — not more alcohol. I'm taking you to Alcoholics Anonymous or to the hospital!" That is almost impossible for an "S" type to do. But through the power of the Holy Spirit, they can do so!)

I have watched "S" type mothers and fathers allow their children to walk all over them. In the long run, that does neither the parent nor the child any good. "S" parents cannot understand why their children don't respond the way *they would respond*. It is because they are different — that is why it is so important to understand these personality types! "D," or "I," or "C" children will *never* respond in the same way as an "S" child. It is up to "S" parents to get themselves under control and function in harmony with their child, rather than allowing the child to become the parent, and the parent the child.

I recently counseled in a situation where the dad was a high "I," the mom was a high "S," and the teenage daughter was an extremely high "D." She ran that house! The parents had become her children and she had, for all practical purposes, become their parent. What a terrible thing to do to a child! What a *difficult* thing to do to a child. What an impossible situation in which to put a teenager. Yet it happens thousands of times daily in many homes.

This material is valuable for all personality types, but perhaps none will benefit more than "S" types when they "wake up and smell the coffee." After that, they are in a better position to help themselves not to be a "sucker" any longer.

Percentage of Population

Research seems to indicate that about 30–35% of the general population has this type profile. That is fitting, considering the activities of this personality type make up the most needed segment of our society. You would expect any culture that basically runs as a *service industry* to have many people who have developed these skills to be productive. (Again, God was merciful to give us so many "S" types!)

Biblical Example

Our Biblical example of a high "S" type personality is the Apostle John. (This is the John who wrote the Gospel of John — don't confuse him with John the Baptist!) The Apostle John was the quiet, unassuming apostle whom Jesus loved. You will never find one incident in John's Gospel where he even mentioned his own name. He always referred to himself as "the other disciple." Because he was so concerned that Jesus receive all the glory, honor and praise, he always took a humble, back-seat role to Jesus and the other disciples.

Not a great deal is even known about John, probably just the way he would have preferred it. He wrote three very short letters found at the end of the *Bible* (I, II, III John), and he wrote The Revelation. It is interesting to note that The Revelation displays the full impact of the glory of God. Surely, John was chosen to "reveal" this information because of his own true humility, desiring only that Christ be worshipped and God receive all the glory.

It is also interesting to note that John was the only disciple not to die a martyr's death. He was exiled to the Island of Patmos to live out his days. I cannot prove it, but I'll bet the Roman Emperor who banished him said, "I don't believe in what he stands for, but I'm not going to kill him... he's too nice... Let's just send him away!" (There are some "safety benefits" in being an "S"!)

It is also worth noting that, although the Apostle Peter has received criticism for publicly denying Jesus, John was just as guilty. If you read John 18 carefully, you will notice that John was standing right beside Peter, keeping very *quiet*. Peter denied Jesus verbally. John denied him silently. Both possessed people-oriented personality styles and "caved in" under the pressure of the circumstances.

When Jesus washed the disciples' feet, he was certainly showing characteristics of a servant. Most of us would not consider stooping so low as to wash someone else's feet. Although this was a custom in the Mideast, it has become part of a religious ceremony that is still used in some churches today. It is an act of personal humility to show yourself willing to care for the needs of others. If the Son of God was willing to "stoop low" to help others, should we not have the same attitude? This will be easy to do for a person with a similar personality. In other words, a high "S" individual would be more prone to this type of service. Even high "I's" might enjoy it because it might make them feel good inside or look good to others. "D" or "C" type personalities would have a little more trouble with it because they are "task" oriented, rather than "people" oriented. They would simply feel that if you wanted clean feet, you should go take a bath!

Again, it is not that one personality type is qualified to serve and another isn't. It is just easier for certain types to follow certain patterns. At the same time, it is more difficult for them to want to do other activities. (In fact, it might be more "sacrificial" for other personality types to move outside their own "comfort zone" in service to God and man, than to stay within their comfortable, self-imposed limitations and perform a service that "just comes naturally" to that type.) Regardless of our profile pattern, we should be willing to submit ourselves to the needs of others, in order that we may help them.

Personal Illustration

My third-born daughter, Elizabeth, has a high "S" type personality. She came home from school when she was in the fourth grade and said, "Daddy, a boy asked me to go steady today." To an adult, it is silly to go steady in the fourth grade — but not when you're *in* the fourth grade. So I asked, "What did you tell him?" She replied, "Well, I told him yes." I asked, "Do you like him?" She said, "No." "Then why did you say you would go steady with him?", I asked. She said, "I didn't want to hurt his feelings!"

I saw my opportunity, and said, "Elizabeth, do you remember when we did your personality profile — "S": **sweet**, **soft**, **stable**, **steady**, **shy**, **status-quo**, **submissive sucker**—do you remember that?" With her big eyes, she looked at me and said, "Yes, sir..." I said, "That is what this is all about. You can't go through life trying to please people. You have to go through life trying to please God." I told Elizabeth to go back to school the next day and tell that little boy that she accepted him and that he was a nice person but that she didn't want to go steady with him anymore. When she got home from school, she told me what she had done. I asked, "What did he say?" She reported, "He looked at me and said, 'That's okay!' and ran off to play." (I thought to myself, "And *she* was worried about *his* feelings?!?") I hugged her and said,

"Elizabeth, you always tend to be a people-pleaser. Don't let people run over you."

It is amazing, because to this day she tells me, "Daddy, I can't count the number of times I have been able to say 'no' because I knew it was wrong. I wanted to do it to please somebody, but I was able to walk away because I understand myself." After you begin to understand yourself, you can begin to let God be in control of you and give you great wisdom.

One night, Elizabeth came home from baby-sitting some neighborhood kids. She told me something unusual had happened. "Daddy, when I told the children to go to bed, they would not obey me. I guess they could sense I was a high 'S' and they wanted to take advantage of me." (By the way, that's really true. No one can "read" you as well as small children. They discover quickly just how far they can push.) Elizabeth continued, "I thought to myself — I can't lose control of this situation. I thought I would use the personality stuff you taught me. I looked at those children, and I *lowered my 'S' and I raised my 'D'* and I told them, 'Your mother and father left me in charge, and they told me to make sure you went to bed at nine o'clock. If you don't get in bed right now, I'm going to tell your parents you wouldn't obey what they said, and you will be in big trouble!'" Elizabeth said they looked at her and said, "Okay — we'll go to bed." And they did! Then she said to me, "You know something, Daddy? That was hard for me to do... but it worked!" I gave her a hug and said, "There are lots of adults who wouldn't have known how to handle that situation. I am very proud of you!"

I couldn't help but think to myself how valuable that information was to Elizabeth, and how well she had used it in a practical way. She lowered her "S" (she didn't want to be a sucker) and raised her "D" (she had to be dominant in the situation), and took charge in a loving manner. I also thought about the thousands of young people (especially "S" types), who would go through life being "run over" by other people, simply because they didn't know how to handle daily situations involving pressure. I can assure you that after you understand this information, teach it to your children and they begin to practice it, you will see life-transforming results.

Basic Need

The basic need of the "S" type personality is *appreciation.* They need to feel needed. Remember Anne Murray's song, "You Needed Me"? Well, "S" types enjoy being helpful, needed and appreciated. High "S's" are a lot like the Pillsbury Dough Boy. When he is pushed in the belly, he smiles and "coos." It makes him feel so loved and appreciated. "S" types are like that — they purr when "stroked," just like a cat.

By the way, it is interesting to note how personality types hear the same words in a different manner. If you tell "S" types, "I appreciate you," they respond with a smile and a "thank you." Tell "D's" you appreciate them and they will quickly respond, "You ought to! As much as I do for you. There are a lot of people who would be grateful to have someone around like me!" High "I's" will respond, "Well, what do I win? Is there some kind of prize that goes along with being appreciated?" The "C's" will wonder, "Am I being manipulated? Are you trying to get something by me? Hmmmmm, what's going on here?" Again, everyone hears the same words, but all interpret them differently. That's because people are different. Are you getting the picture?

Strengths

The high "S" is easygoing. He likes life to be like a calm lake, rather than a turbulent ocean. Neither does he like to "make waves"! He likes life to flow at an even, steady pace. Remember, both "S's" and "I's" are people-oriented. They have a built-in radar detector to focus on the needs, feelings, and desires of other people. The high "I" is outgoing. The high "S" is more reserved in nature.

"S's" are dependable. They love routine because it makes them feel comfortable. They do not like surprises. They prefer the standard, tried and proven method of doing things. Thus they are dependable because of their strong affinity for sameness. After they have done a task several times, it becomes a part of their nature and they feel very uncomfortable if things move outside of the "known" or threaten to change.

Even though "S's" are reserved, they make good leaders. They lead as a coach, rather than as a dictator. If they run a company, they do more than *tell* employees what to do — they are willing to *show* them. They feel like parents to their employees, as well as everyone else they meet. "S" types have an inner desire to rescue people from their troubles. This is commendable; however, they should exhibit cautiousness because they have such big hearts. Sometimes they become "easy marks" and are easily taken advantage of. This doesn't bother high "S's" — they feel everything will "even out" in the long run... and they are probably right.

An "S" is very orderly and efficient, preferring to know that things are running smoothly. One of their mottos is, "Working together we can do it." They may not always accomplish that goal but they would like to. It's a feeling that stays with them constantly.

"S's" are very practical. They look for the simplest solution. When coloring a picture, they feel it is important to stay inside the lines. Again, tried and proven methods are their norm. It is possible for them to break out into unknown territory and do things they have never done before. However, it is extremely uncomfortable for them to do so.

Naturally, we would expect the "S" type to be conservative. "S's" like to stick with things they know will work. Their dress, manners, religion, politics, business investments, etc., are all done on a conservative basis.

Again, this is one reason that understanding different personality types is so important. Anyone running for public office, anyone preaching or speaking, anyone involved in sales — and most importantly, anyone *parenting* — should remember that there are at least four primary points-of-view on any one topic. If you simply present your own view, you will have only a 10% to 35% chance of hitting your target audience, according to the percentage of the population that also sees things your way. However, if you try to cover your topic with four views in mind (i.e., trying to respond to the different basic needs of D-I-S-C styles), you can significantly increase your level of productivity, communication and understanding.

The high "S" is a diplomat with people. Because they are so flexible, they are enjoyable to be around. They are able to see things from everyone's point of view. In a scene from "The Fiddler on the Roof," a man makes a political statement to Tevya, the local dairy farmer. Tevya responds, "You are right!"

Soon, an opposing political statement is made. Again, Tevya responds, "You are right!" Then a wise guy says, "Wait a minute! First you say *this* man is right; now you say the *other* one is right. They can't *both* be right!" Tevya answers: "You know something? *You* are right, too!" Such is the ability of the high "S."

"S's" can be extremely humorous. Their reserved, dry humor helps them see the lighter side of life. They are curious, wanting to know what is going on and who is doing what — keeping up with all the current news on everybody. Usually they know all the latest fads. Because they like to please people, they try to keep up with current trends. Even though "S" types prefer to stay in the background, their presence can always be felt. Without them, "D's," "I's" and "C's" wouldn't have anyone to push around!

Weaknesses

As with every personality type, weaknesses are simply strengths taken too far, and thus abused. Most of the time we operate on the basis of our strengths. We are most within our "comfort zone" when we allow ourselves to function in harmony with our own feelings and personality. For example, "S's" are most comfortable while functioning as **sweet, soft, stable, steady, shy, status-quo, sentimental, submissive** individuals. When their environment or circumstances change, they may feel they are in "hostile territory." Suddenly, they may feel "put upon." That is the time their weakness has the greatest opportunity to manifest itself. It is precisely at that moment, as with all personality types, that one should focus on staying under control, and not become susceptible to the natural tendencies of forceful personality weaknesses.

"S's" can be very **stingy**. They like their own space. When someone suddenly invades their territory, they may feel they are losing ground. It's not so much that they don't want to share their possessions with others, but they don't want to lose the stability of knowing their boundaries. They like to know what is theirs and what is not. In other words, they fear losing their **security**.

"S" types, perhaps more than any other, can become fearful at times. They don't like unknown situations at all. They much prefer proven procedures. In other words, they want to know the outcome before they start. They prefer situations that are reliable and predictable. When things drift out of their arena of the "familiar," they become very uncomfortable. They do not like the "fly-by-the-seat-of-your-pants" attitude of the high "D" or "I." A few years back, there was a popular song entitled, "Don't Rock the Boat, Baby." That's precisely how the "S" type feels.

"S's" can be very indecisive. When you ask them a question, they usually give two or three answers. They don't like being wrong, nor do they want to create disharmony. They try to give *the answer they think you want to hear.* When you ask, "Which restaurant would you like to go to for dinner?", they will probably respond, "It doesn't matter — wherever you want is fine with me." Remember, as with the "I," these two types are "people pleasers." It is not so much that they have a hard time making up their minds as it is that they try to guess where you are coming from with your question so they can answer appropriately.

Dr. Gary Chapman tells the story of how he trained a man, who was having difficulty communicating with his wife, to listen better by simply repeating her previous statements back to her in the form of a question, to clarify things. When the man got home, his wife said, "You sure look tired." He replied, "Are you saying I look tired?" She said, "I don't know if *you're* tired or if *I'm* tired." He asked, "Are you saying *you* feel tired?" She said, "I don't know if I'm tired, or whether I just feel cooped up in this house. We never go anywhere or do anything anymore!" He responded, "Are you feeling like you would like to get out of the house and maybe go out and do something?" She said, "Maybe if we could go out to eat I would feel better." He asked, "Are you saying you would like to go out to eat?" She said, "I know our finances are tight right now and we can't afford to go out to eat, but maybe if we could go get dessert somewhere, I'd feel better." He said, "Are you saying you would like to go out and get dessert somewhere?" She said, "Could we?" And off they went — happy together! Dr. Chapman points out, "Not only did the *husband* not know where his wife was going with her statements, *she* probably didn't know, either!"

It is hard to interpret "Could we go get dessert?" out of "You sure look tired!" Unfortunately, this is just the way we all are made. When an "S" type (or any type) is being indecisive, just be patient. They will "come around" in a few minutes. Ask a few questions and show a lot of love — we all have our moments!

Another reason "S" types appear to be indecisive goes back to their preference for decisions that have predictable outcomes. If they don't know *how* their choice will affect other people, they may "freeze up" and try to put off the decision. It's not because they *can't* make up their minds — they just don't want to see anyone hurt or left out.

"S" types appear to be **spectators**, and they certainly don't want to create a conflict. They usually don't raise their hands or try to be "pushy" when it comes to being recognized. They prefer to be part of a group activity much more than being in the spotlight alone. They enjoy watching others being involved in activities, but prefer not embarrassing themselves publicly if at all possible.

You can see how potentially devastating it could be for a High "S" parent to try to rear a child who is a strong "D" or "I." Left unchecked, that child would soon become the parent, and the parent would take on characteristics of a child. It would *wear* on the parent constantly to deal with someone who is more aggressive and outgoing than themselves. The parent should not look at this situation as a threat of personal confrontation. It is just a difference in personality style. When parents understand that their child is not trying to be rebellious, but is simply allowing his personality style to get the upper hand, they can nurture and guide him so his "pushiness" can be overcome and is not offensive to adults. Parents shouldn't "cave in" at times like this, but try to be loving yet firm in teaching the child what is taking place. After the information has been imparted, the child will have a better opportunity to mature properly.

Often, "S" types seem to be **self-protective**. They fear being humiliated. Because they have such a hard time saying "no" to others, they try to position themselves so they won't let you down or disappoint you. They sometimes maneuver circumstances carefully in order to protect themselves. They do so in a manner which is passive in nature, rather than confrontational.

Lack of motivation sometimes is a weakness of the "S" type. Because they tend to be more reserved than the "I" type, and less task-oriented than the "C" type, they stand back and wait to be told what to do. They would rather do nothing than do something wrong. They may give up out of frustration if they fail to be appreciated or properly directed. However, they often go the second, third or fourth mile if you give them direction. It is important to learn the value of risk and the importance of being a self-starter. After all, "nothing ventured, nothing gained!"

Every so often, I meet a couple with one child, and the child happens to have an "S" personality. Usually, "S" types are much easier to raise than others. (Sorry, you can't place an order for what personality type you want in your children. You get what comes!) When these parents hear other couples talking about struggles in raising children, they wonder what they mean. To them, rearing children isn't hard at all. That's when I pray, "Dear Lord, please allow all of their birth control methods to fail and send them *triplet* 'D's!' Then they will know what parenting is all about!"

Finally, "S" types sometimes appear to become **selfish.** It is not so much that they must have their own way; they are just trying to protect their own interests and stability. The three other personality types ("D," "I" and "C") know it is important to look out for yourself, while "S" types tend to help others before they help themselves. But after "getting burned" a few times, they begin to get the picture and try to be more cautious. They use a very low-key approach to life, making sure others cannot detect that they are really protecting their own interests. Usually, if they don't look out for themselves, no one else will either.

"S's" Make Good:

High "S" personality types make excellent diplomats. They have a natural ability to see things from everyone's perspective. They have a way of opening the eyes of others, to try to create a more harmonious atmosphere and relationship for all concerned. Their kindhearted ways make them feel that real understanding is truly possible between all people, if only we would take time to listen and learn from each other.

Perhaps the most common profession in which to find "S's" is among school teachers. After all, if there was ever a "helping profession," surely it is teaching! Early hours, meetings, lessons to prepare, papers to grade, phone calls to make, more meetings, tests to design, late hours, and finally *more* meetings, are not uncommon for teachers. They must be equipped to withstand such a lifestyle. (I have often said there will be a special section in heaven for teachers... no students allowed!)

"S" types also make excellent technicians, such as nurses. They are dedicated and dependable. They seek to do all they can to help and to please their patients, and to make them as comfortable as possible. They are able to "put themselves in your situation" better than the other personality types. This is why they seem so sweet to others.

"S's" make good accountants or bank tellers. They enjoy the steady, stable routine lifestyle that comes with banking procedures. The daily rituals of opening and closing on time, talking to customers, and handling the same routine matters — all these appeal to them.

Finally, "S's" make excellent secretaries. They are very people-oriented, so they greet the public well. They are also a little more reserved, so they are able to stay at their desks and get their work done. Personally, I try to find a high "S" when hiring a secretary for two reasons: First, High "S's" are great finishers. They really enjoy seeing a project completed. The second reason is because I once had a "D" type secretary. When I gave her something to do, she would *correct* it... and *give it back* to me! I often wondered, "Who is working for whom?" By the way, I once had a high "C" secretary who did excellent, excellent work. But I always had to remind her to take time to be friendly and outgoing. People are not interruptions — people are our business!

And to make my story complete, let me tell you about my onetime high "I" secretary. I never could keep up with her. I gave her work to do, she put it on her desk, and then went "visiting" around the office. She was absolutely fantastic with people. She just never got her work done. At the end of each day, I had a talk with her about her work habits. Looking back, I could have saved myself many hours of frustration (not to mention stress and anger!) if I had only understood where each secretary was coming from. I didn't understand personality types years ago, so I always hired on the basis of *what I saw,* rather than what was really present.

I should have figured this out as a school principal. The students had discovered more about a teacher's ability in the classroom after 10 minutes than I could through interviewing a prospective teacher for 10 hours. It is not what you *see* that counts — it is what is *really* there! "Average" kids often can see through to the truth faster than "sophisticated" adults.

I should note again that I am not trying to "pigeon hole" personality types. Certain jobs are better-suited to some individuals than others — but personality traits and skills do not determine if a person is "good" or "bad." While we say that someone is "the wrong person for the job," it is actually the *job* that may not be right for that *person.* Any personality type can

POSITIVE PERSONALITY PROFILES

make a great secretary, but regardless of the type, we need to understand the *job* and *ourselves* to be successful and fulfilled.

Review

High "S" type personalities make **sweet** individuals. When dealing with them, you will find they are a delight to all other personality types. Who wouldn't be attracted to people who go out of their way to do almost anything for you? "S" types are happiest when *you* are happy. If someone gets "the short end of the stick," it is often them, but they don't mind. They just don't want anyone else to suffer.

It is important that the "D's," "I's," and "C's" realize that "S" types are easily taken advantage of. We should all do our part to be supportive of them. Also, it is important that "S" types not allow themselves to be abused. If you are an "S" type in an abusive situation, please seek help. You do not need to be abused. Also avoid the trap of becoming an enabler — helping those who are sick to remain that way with your help. Often, when people are sick they find someone who will give them "strokes." Strokes feel good; therefore, more strokes are required. Soon, a vicious, downhill spiral has begun: sickness, reinforcement ("S" offering support), lack of desire to get better, more reinforcement from further support and concern, more sickness, more caring and sharing — and soon, both become sick! With proper help and counseling, the cycle can be broken.

"S" types are the **salt** of the earth. If we didn't have them, we would all be poorer indeed.

Chapter Five:

The "C" Type Personality

Our "C" type personality is both *reserved* and *task-oriented*. Keep a mental image where this type falls in our model of human behavior (unshaded area noted by the question mark).

The "C" types are **competent** individuals. They *know* that they *know* what they *know!* They have done their homework. They research the facts and follow them carefully. They develop a plan of action and follow it. Their motto could be, "Plan your work… work your plan!"

"C's" are fairly **cautious**. They look before they leap. Their target practice slogan might be, "Ready… Aim… Aim… Aim…!" They don't like making mistakes. "Measure twice, cut once."

"C's" are **careful**. They proofread Xerox copies! Well, they are not actually that careful, but you get the point — they really like to make sure things are done carefully.

The "C" types are **calculating**. Because they are task-oriented, they tend to think in terms of the "bottom line." They will be the first to explain basic economics to you: "If your outgo exceeds your income, your upkeep will be your downfall!"

"C's" are known for their ability to use **critical thinking**. They can analyze a situation perhaps better than any of the other types. They have an uncanny ability to "see behind the scenes" and understand what is really going on. I was getting involved in a business deal one time and my wife, Donna, a "C," asked me not to. She discerned something wrong with the group's general partner. Did I listen to her? No. I should have — she was right. It was a costly mistake. I learned my lesson.

"C's" demand **compliance**. *They* follow instructions and can't understand why *others* won't do the same... and just *do* what they're *supposed* to do. A High "C" originated the phrase, "If all else fails, follow the directions!"

The "C" type is not pushy, and does not need to be the group leader. It is okay with them simply to follow along and have a good time — as long as they are having a *good* time, and not a *dangerous* time! They enjoy being around others who are outgoing. They like the way "D's" and "I's" make fools of themselves — just don't ask *them* to do it. They don't mind if they don't get all the credit for a good job they did, but don't try giving them all the blame, either! They will "fold" on you.

"C's" are extremely **conscientious**. They can stay on track with a project long after others have given up. They enjoy putting together jigsaw or crossword puzzles. They see things fall into place step-by-step. They have little time for "horsing around." Most of life is serious to them. As Sergeant Friday used to say on "Dragnet": "Just the facts, ma'am — just the facts!"

High "C's" love detail. High "S's" love detail as it relates to people, but no one enjoys knowing every little intimate detail about everything as much as a high "C." I have a friend who was at home one Saturday when his high "C" wife told him she was going to the shopping mall. He decided to keep a detailed list of everything that occurred while she was gone, because he knew that when she came home, she would ask what had happened. He was excited at the prospect of his new-found project.

The process and list began: "One o'clock: watched 'Bonanza.' Little Joe and Hoss went into town and got into a fight. Two o'clock: watched 'The Rifleman.' Lucas McCain and Mark went into town on their wagon. Two-thirty: watched Roy Rogers and Dale Evans. Two-forty-five: your brother called. He wanted to tell you he would see you in a few weeks at the family get-together." On and on he went, writing down everything that happened that afternoon. Finally around six o'clock, his wife walked into the house and asked (as he expected), "What all happened while I was gone?" She had fallen right into his trap!

He started through his list: "One o'clock: watched 'Bonanza.' Little Joe and Hoss went into town and got into a fight. Two o'clock: watched 'The Rifleman.' Lucas McCain and Mark went into town..." He said it took him about 10 minutes to slowly and carefully read through his chronology, afraid to look up in the process because he knew he would start laughing. When he finished, he said he looked up and his wife had tears running down her cheeks. She looked at him and said, "You *do* love me, don't you!?" She was thrilled by what he had done, rather than offended by it. It was her "language of love," seeing how much he cared in giving her details about what happened in his day. Sometimes you just can't win!

"C's" love to be **correct** — not because they think they are better than other people. They just enjoy being right. To them, "any job worth doing at all is worth doing well." They feel like their work makes a statement about themselves; therefore, it should be correct. You can count on the "C" type being right about almost any topic most of the time.

I was speaking at a convention of mobile home park managers. I kept referring to their place of business as a "trailer park." During a break, one gentleman shared with me that the phrase "trailer park" was really inaccurate. He told me they viewed themselves as "mobile home" managers — that a "trailer" is what you pull on the back of a car, but what you live in is a mobile home. After the break, I used this information as a wonderful illustration of how important it is to adjust your style in order not to offend other people. During the rest of the seminar, I referred to all of the individuals in attendance as "mobile home managers." They smiled each time I said that, understanding that I knew where they were coming from. They observed how I had adjusted my style to have better communications with them.

My mind reflected back to the time I went on my first cruise. I was talking to the captain and asked him what was the length of the "boat." He looked at me, and asked incredulously: "The *boat?*" I responded, "Yes, what is the length of this boat?" Indignant, he replied, "A *boat* is what you fish in — *this* is a *ship!*" I realized that I had called his beloved by the wrong name. Of course, from now on, whenever I am on a large sea vessel, I refer to it as a "ship," and not a "boat." Again, these are simple illustrations, but they point out how words that don't mean much to us can be very important (at best) and even inflammatory (at worst) to other individuals.

"C's" tend to be **conformists**, especially when it comes to going along with the tried-and-proven. However, if they think they can better a situation, they will make every effort to do so. "Build a better mousetrap and the world will beat a path to your door." A "C" type thought that up! They look for ways to take information we already possess and improve on it.

"C" types like to keep things under their **control**. That way, they always know what's going on. One night, when my wife was in the kitchen making the children's lunches for school, I reached down to grab a few potato chips and she told me I couldn't have any! I thought to myself, "Wait a minute... I paid for these! Why can't I eat some?" She explained that she had divided them out for the children's lunches, and that she would be happy to buy some extra chips next time if I wanted some. I thought that was ridiculous — I couldn't even have a few chips! I tossed them back in the bag and walked out of the kitchen as I muttered, "Picky, picky, picky!"

Well, time passed and our busy family got busier. I volunteered to start making the children's lunches. One night, while I was making sandwiches and putting cookies and chips in the bag, Rachael and Esther came into the kitchen and started talking to me... while munching on the chips. As I watched the bag begin to dwindle, I said, "Wait a minute — you can't eat those chips! I won't have any to pack in your lunch." They said, "Dad... we can't have any chips?" I replied, "That isn't the issue. You can have all the chips you want, but if you eat them, I won't have any to pack in your lunches." They looked at me, tossed the handful back in the bag and walked out of the room as they murmured, "Picky, picky, picky!"

Suddenly, I thought to myself, "Hey, I've seen this movie

before!" The light clicked on in my mind — oh, so that's what she meant! I went and told my wife what happened… and apologized for not "hearing" her earlier. By the way, if you are ever at our house for a meal, we will share everything we have with you… Just don't eat the chips!

I "raised my 'C'" a great deal in preparing this book. It took planning, preparation, and short-term interval goals to complete it. When you focus on your "C" traits, you can figure a better way to do just about anything. I had read, studied and heard much on different personality types, but not in a way I could understand. I reworked the material, added personal research and insights, repackaged it, and tried a new method. So far, so good! (By the way, thank you for buying a copy!)

"C" types are **convinced**. They love to be accurate — they know what it means to "do your homework." If they are sure they are right, there is no changing their minds. You may think you can persuade them differently, but that is simply not the case. "He who is convinced against his will is of the same opinion still." That really applies to a "C."

Finally, "C's" are very **consistent**. You can set your watch by them. You can usually go to the bank on what they tell you. They are hardly ever incorrect in the details of a story. Like the "S," they love doing things the same way. If it worked once, why change it? They feel better about repetition than the "D" or the "I," who interject change often. "Variety is the spice of life" to "D's" and "I's." To a "C," variety can be dangerous — better to stick with what you know, be safe, be consistent. By the way, "C's" usually make good parents because they are so consistent with their children. The kids may not always agree, but they always know where their parents stand!

Percentage of Population

Research seems to indicate that about 20–25% of the general population has a high "C" profile. This fits accurately with regard to the number of physicians, lawyers, professors, and inventors we have in our society. "C" types are so smart. They can do just about anything they put their minds to. They are not the majority of the population, but they are strong enough in number to let us know they exist and are ready to help! "C" types usually have figured out a way to have a pretty good income, too!

Biblical Example

A Biblical example of the high "C" profile is also found in one of the twelve disciples, Thomas. You remember, when Jesus arose from the dead others said, "Thomas, we have seen the Lord." Thomas replied, "Right — dead people get up every day!" (All right, I have taken some liberties with the Greek text...! But, basically, that was Thomas' reply.) Does his response sound like the words of one who followed Jesus faithfully for three and a half years, or does it sound like words of an atheist? "I do not believe Jesus has risen from the grave. Unless I see for myself, I will not believe!"

Still more amazing is that, when Jesus appeared to his disciples eight days later, he didn't tell Thomas, "I am so ashamed of you. How could you, one of my chosen, let me down?" In John 20, Jesus said (again taking some liberties in paraphrasing): "Thomas, come here... I understand you, and I perceive that you are a high 'C.' I know you have an inquisitive mind. I understand you have questions... So come here. I am going to give you some *tangible* answers. Touch me and feel me.

I am not a ghost." Thomas fell on his face and said, "My Lord and my God!" Jesus said, "Thomas, because you have seen me you have believed. Blessed are they who have not seen and yet believe" (John 20:29). He didn't chide him; he gave Thomas what "C's" need: quality answers!

Personal Illustration

When my wife and I were dating, I read her all wrong — and she read me all wrong, too! Actually, someone has noted that dating is one of the most deceitful times of our entire life. We do everything in our power to fool the other person into thinking we are somehow perfect. Bad news — "Prince Charming" and "Snow White" are the only couple that "lived happily ever after..." and they are both dead!

I was dating Donna, and she seemed to have so many questions. I thought to myself, "This girl thinks I know everything. I had better marry her quickly, before she finds out any differently!" She was thinking, "This guy is the most fun in the world. I should marry him before he finds out I'm a little afraid of people." So, we got married. Her questions continued — but now they sounded totally different.

I can remember one day I came home and said, "We're going to Florida on a vacation." She asked, "Do you have a map?" I said, "Who needs a map...? I know where Florida is, it's below Georgia somewhere — we'll find it!" She asked, "Have you made a hotel reservation yet?" I said, "There are hotels everywhere — we'll find one!" She asked, "How many miles will we go the first day before we stop?" I whined, "I don't know. I don't even *want* to go to Florida now. You've taken all the fun out of it for me!"

Rather than realizing her questions revealed an inquiring mind, I felt she was nagging. And to her, all my "fun" suddenly seemed like irresponsible behavior. We were stuck! Things were not unbearable — they just weren't great. (I guess you could say things were average — just as near the bottom as they were near the top.) We had both hoped (and assumed falsely) that they would be perfect.

Finally in 1985, after 15 years of marriage, I began to learn how to apply this material. I took it from the theoretical to the practical — from my head to my daily life. I tried speaking *her* "language of love" — *quality answers* and *details*. Almost overnight, things started to improve. She began to learn about me and began to give me some *recognition*. We started "becoming one" for the first time. We actually learned that the other half of us — our "missing half," although very different — is very important. I think better with her. She has more fun because of me. We are now a team. We started out all wrong and went about building our marriage the hard way. Now we are working smarter... not harder... and definitely better!

Basic Need

The basic need of the high "C" personality is *quality answers*. You can give "C's" an answer, but if it's not a *very good* answer, to them it is no answer at all! It must be an answer with quality components. For example, when a "C" asks you, "When are we leaving?", he doesn't want to hear, "Tomorrow." He prefers, "We will leave tomorrow at three o'clock p.m. You must be packed and ready to be picked up by one-fifteen, sharp! You can take two suitcases and one carry-on bag. That will give us 45 minutes to get to the airport, and one hour to get through the security check and to the gate. I will see you at one-fifteen!"

Even after all of that, he will still probably ask, "Are you *sure* you are allowing enough time?"

Strengths

The "C" type personality is usually extremely gifted. They are very bright and have a high capacity for intellectual achievement. They have minds that think in terms of "a better idea." Although they can be very creative, they often shine by taking an already proven idea and building upon it. They have an inventor's mind and instinct.

"C's" are very analytical. They know how to take a big project and break it down into little components. Unfortunately, they sometimes struggle to see "the big picture" when working with all the little pieces. They tend to bog down in detail. In other words, they are excellent at *analyzing* (seeing the details) but often poor at *synthesizing* (seeing the overall big picture).

"C" types tend to be very sensitive. They are seldom wrong. They often double-check themselves to make sure they are correct. If they are in error, they take it rather personally. They know they are not perfect, but they hate to admit it. It "rubs them the wrong way" when someone comes along and points out an error they have made.

The "C" type has the attitude of a perfectionist. As I said before, they proofread Xerox copies! They love documentation and accuracy. My high school English teacher had a reputation for being tough. I worked especially hard on my first paper, trying to get off to a good start. I was shocked when I got it back — a "D"! She wrote a note: "Your grammar was good but you had poor mechanics. You did not dot your 'i's' over the correct place and you crossed your 't's' through more letters than just the 't.'"

Unbelievable! I couldn't understand it then, but I do now. She was a high "C" looking for carefulness and correctness. I was a high "I" thinking she should be happy that I even turned the paper in on time! After that first bad experience, I basically "quit" on her for the rest of the year. What a waste! If she, as an adult educator, had known how to "prime" me, I would have learned much more. Would it have been so hard for her to write: "Good wording! You are off to a good start. Be sure to use careful punctuation dotting 'i's' and crossing 't's.' Attention to these details will help you even more. I did not penalize you this first time — now you know. I am excited about watching you progress in my class this year!" I would have "charged hell" with a water pistol for her! She didn't understand me — I didn't understand me *or* her! As educators, we must do all we can to help our students. (See Chapter 10 for further help.)

There is an old saying: "The teacher has not taught anything until the student has learned." The first time I heard that statement, I didn't like it. I have since come to agree with it. It puts the burden for learning on the shoulders of the teacher. We are the adults. Oftentimes, we hold the keys to a student's academic success or failure, whether we want to admit it or not. It may be true that children do not make up 100% of our population, but they do make up 100% of our future!

It is not uncommon for "C's" to be extremely aesthetic. They are often "as neat as a pin." To them, external appearance is a statement of internal condition. Everything must be as organized as possible. After all, "a messy desk reveals a messy mind."

"C's" are very idealistic — perhaps too much so. They want to be the best, look for the best, and strive for the best. They like things to fit together in a nice, neat package. The "loose ends" of the world frustrate them. They try to bring closure to all of their experiences. They don't like things to end abruptly or unexpectedly. They are strong, cognitive processors, and they expect others to be the same. They love the television game show, "Jeopardy!" because it is hard but fair. They think ideally that is the way life should be — hard, but fair. It frustrates "C's" to discover life is really more like "Wheel of Fortune" — simple and silly! (Most high "I's" think "Wheel of Fortune" is great — they will not even watch "Jeopardy!" They don't know any of the answers.)

"C" types are loyal to ideas and traditions. They find what they like and stick to it. Because they are so consistent, they enjoy being in a familiar "comfort zone." But when "C's" find themselves in unknown territory, they feel threatened. Their personal loyalty pretty much goes right out the window! We could say they are loyal as long as they know all the details of the plan. But when details unravel, so does their loyalty.

Finally, "C" types are very self-sacrificing and tenacious. They have the enviable ability to "stick with the stuff." They constantly look for ways to make a situation better. They work tirelessly to do a good job. They have a desire to do quality work and do so even when it means long, hard hours. They usually put the task-at-hand ahead of their own personal well-being. "C's" have been known to operate on nervous energy long past their bedtime.

Weaknesses

The "C" types can be very self-centered. This is because

they are always right — well, at least they *think* they are. (The word *think* is emphasized to remind us how cognitive they are in their personality style. They really use their minds — perhaps more so than any of the other personality styles. They say "I know that..." or "I think that...", while others are more likely to say "I feel that..." or "It sounds to me that..." or "It looks like...")

While "C" types usually are correct in the decisions they make, unfortunately, they let you know about it. They have myopic vision (can only see things close-up), and often they lack the flexibility to develop warm, interpersonal relationships. In other words, their way is the best way — and often the only way.

"C's" can often be very moody. Their "feelers" are off-kilter a little bit; therefore, they *react* more to their environment, rather than *responding* to it. If they get in a tough spot, they tend to react negatively and very quickly so! They don't respond well to being told they made an error, or are wrong. They have a great desire always to be right. That is a heavy burden to carry, but they do carry it. Their disposition will change quickly if they are corrected. You will often think, "Why are they so moody?"

Perhaps the most difficult aspect of a "C's" life is the way they deal with their negative, critical nature. Rather than keeping it under control, it is often out of control. Even though they are intelligent and have much to offer, they often "cut off their own nose" by not warming up to a situation before making their recommendations and comments. In other words, they are known as "faultfinders." They tend to see what is wrong, rather than what is right. They see the glass as being half-empty, rather than being half-full.

I have a friend who says his mother was definitely a "C" type. He told me he brought home a "B" on his report card and his mother said, "Son, you could have made an 'A.'" Next grading period, he made an "A." His mother looked at his report card and said, "Son, you could have made an 'A+.'" Next time, he made an "A+." He was so proud of himself. He ran home and showed her his report card. She took one look at it and said, "Son, you could have taken a harder course!" Are "C's" perfectionists or what!?!

Have you ever seen the game in a magazine or newspaper, "What's Wrong With This Picture?" It was designed by a "C" type personality. If they would "get a grip," they could see how they are their own worst enemies. Most people are open to innovative ideas the "C" type has to offer. However, because the "C's" misread people, they cannot understand why others don't see the value and wisdom in their ideas. What they fail to see is that people are not rejecting their *ideas* — people are actually rejecting *them*. They come across so superior in their knowledge that, even when they are right, others don't like to admit it. Do most people like someone who seems to be a "know-it-all"?

Another weakness of the "C" is a rigid nature. Oddly enough, the "C" type has the most difficulty understanding the concepts in this book. It is not because they can't process it mentally — far from it. They just don't believe it is necessary. After all, they have the most trouble understanding why others can't view things as they do. Their rigidity and fear of being wrong keep them from seeing the bigger picture.

"C's" are theoretical in nature. They think their ideas, views and opinions should be the norm. Henry Ford was once told that Chevrolet was planning to offer customers a choice of colors in the following year's model. Ford's executives were concerned that people would like variety and went to him with their concerns. His theorized that people were accustomed to "basic black" and preferred to stick with what they already knew. When management pursued the issue, Ford commented, "They can have their choices — between 'basic black' or 'basic black.'" Well, that year Chevrolet offered colors and the American public responded. The rest is history: Chevrolet outsold Ford that year, and every year thereafter. Henry Ford's theory was great — to him. It just wasn't that great to everyone else.

"C" types can be impractical at times. They know the shortest distance between two points is a straight line; therefore, that principal should *always* work. Unfortunately, life has its way of providing us with detours we are not expecting. "C's" will continue to press an issue long after there is any value in discussing the matter further. Sometimes, their impractical nature keeps them from being heard, even when they have really good ideas.

"C" types tend to be unsociable. They are task-oriented and see little value in "warm fuzzies." Rather than socialize, they would prefer to work on their latest project, to do paperwork at home or at the office, or to read a good book. They often are promoted at work because they do such an excellent job, rather than because they are so well-liked.

"C's" like to protect themselves. They do not take risks, because they might fail. "C's" don't like to make mistakes, and sometimes even taking a safe, calculated risk can mean failure. It is easier for a "C" to stay on "safe ground" and criticize others who venture into unknown territory. This is unfortunate, because many "C's" have outstanding minds, and if they were not afraid of a little risk, assets would far outweigh liabilities.

Finally, "C" types can be extremely vengeful. If they want to get even with you for something you have done, they can be very patient, waiting for just the right moment to help you hang yourself. It is especially difficult for a "C" type to go through any kind of counseling or therapy for personal problems. To them, *you* may have a problem, but they do not — and that is their biggest problem of all. *They are so right, they are wrong!* If you ever tell them how you really feel toward them, they may hold it against you forever. They do not easily forgive anyone who wrongs them.

"C's" Make Good:

"C" types do well in a variety of professions. Perhaps more than any of the other personalities, "C" types can do just about anything because they are so intelligent (**cognitive**). They make excellent teachers or professors because they know so much. They are so factual in their information. They sometimes have difficulty in communicating what they know because they tend to be more reserved than outgoing... and more technical than entertaining. The high "C/I" combination makes one of the best teaching styles, because the information is accurate while the delivery is fun and exciting. (However, it is an unusual and difficult combination to find.)

"C's" also make great inventors or researchers. They have the ability to do several hundred experiments without giving up in the search for a solution. Thomas Edison was asked if he was ever discouraged in his work of inventing the incandescent light bulb — after all, he had tried over 2,000 experiments before beginning to make real progress. He replied, "Not at all, for I knew *for sure* 2,000 ways it would not work!" (It's a good thing this project wasn't assigned to a high "I." We would still be using candles!)

After one of my seminars, a man came up to me who had worked for Edison Industries years ago. He shared with me that in every office there was a picture of Mr. Edison on a plaque bearing this motto: "There is a better way... find it!" He said, humorously, "Sometimes, we would rewrite the saying to read: "There is a way... better find it!" Mr. Edison certainly had the tenacity to "stick with the stuff" until a better way of doing things had been found. This attitude and personal industry has made the world a better place for all of us.

"C's" make excellent musicians. Music has elements of exact science, and they like that. (In other words, you can't play "almost" the right note.) They have the self-discipline required to practice daily and get their songs exactly the way they want them to sound. Also, they make good artists for the same reason. They have an intense desire to create and improve upon life's conditions. They sincerely want the world to be a better place.

"C's" make good philosophers. Their analytical nature gives their theoretical minds the desire to discover the "why" behind everything. Because they know how to "do their homework," when they "philosophize" about something, they are usually correct.

Review

"C" types are cautious, but they have keen eyes. They can spot a good company and purchase its stock while the price is right. They know how to pace themselves. They are not sprinters, but marathon runners. They possess a lot of self-discipline and personal integrity. They see only black or white — with them, not much is gray.

The world will continue to progress as long as we have "C's" making things run more efficiently. The technology of the 21st Century is in the hands of our "C's" friends. Someone has well noted: "D's" create things, "I's" sell them, "S's" enjoy them, and "C's" improve them. "C" types help all of us to be more precise and efficient. Their contributions to our society are priceless. We owe them a great deal of gratitude.

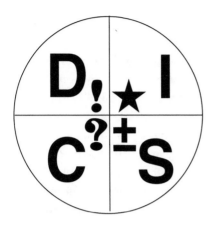

Chapter Six:

Charac-
terizing
Qualities

The different personality types have different natural tendencies. Our tendencies are our "comfort zones" — the areas wherein we feel most comfortable. As we face daily situations, our feelings search out areas of comfort and safety. It is at this point that our "automatic pilot" assumes control, allowing our "natural tendencies" to take over.

The story is told that one day the Lone Ranger and Tonto found themselves surrounded by fierce savages on the warpath. The Masked Rider of the Plains, reloading his revolver with the last of his silver bullets, turned to his faithful Indian companion and said, "Well, this is it! It's been great knowing you. I don't think we can get out of this one..." To which Tonto replied, "What you mean 'we,' Pale Face?" Apparently, when Tonto had to make a decision, he was greatly affected by his natural tendencies!

Let us take a look at some of the natural tendencies of the D–I–S–C personality types. Most misunderstandings occur among the different personality styles as a result of *differences* in perception. If the facts could be laid out clearly, we would see that they are simply that: facts. However, different personality styles *perceive* facts in differing ways. Given the same "facts" concerning an overall project, a "D" type may think, "*What* is going on here?" An "I" type might think, "*Who* all is invited to this function?" An "S" type wonders, "*How* do we need to do this project?", while a "C" type asks, "*Why* are we doing this?" Again, the issue is not so much the actual information or factual data as it is our perception and perspective regarding that information. (The most *natural* thing in all the world is to see things from our own perspective. The most *supernatural* thing in all the world is to see things from someone else's perspective.) Sadly, very few people focus on doing that. If we can learn the secret of seeing things from different perspectives, our interpersonal relationships will broaden, and we will be more tolerant of each other.

Let's see how different personality types respond to situations, based on their own perspectives.

Questions they want answered:

D – What?   As in *what* is the bottom line?
I – Who?   As in *who* will be going?
S – How?   As in *how* do you want this done?
C – Why?   As in *why* are we doing this?

One evening, my wife and I were in the car when our oldest daughter, Rachael, called our mobile phone. She said, "Hi, Dad! Do we have a chain saw?" I replied, "No, but check with Tut, the guy who lives across the street. I think he might have one." After I hung up, my wife asked me what Rachael had wanted. I said, "She just wanted to know if we had a chain saw, but I told her we didn't." Then, with a hint of anxiety in her voice, my wife asked, "Why did she want a chain saw?" And I thought to myself, "I don't know — it never crossed my mind to ask her!" After I shared this thought with her, she grabbed for the phone and called Rachael back — I guess she pictured Rachael hacking through all the bannister railings in the house! To my wife's great relief, Rachael explained that a friend had dropped by and needed one to cut up a tree that had fallen in his yard. The point of this story illustrates how differently the personality types see or think things through. My interest was in *who* had a chain saw, while my wife's was in *why* she would need one. The issue is not which of us was "right." Rather, it demonstrates that we see things through different "filters." In many instances, we can help and complement each other.

In communicating with or approaching anyone, it is a good idea to keep these "filters" in mind. Remember, no one is strictly a "D," or an "I," or an "S" or a "C." We are all combinations of these traits to a greater or lesser degree. So, it stands to reason that it is a good idea to cover all the bases, or at least as many as necessary, to produce understanding and harmony in the communication process. Just the simple effort of *trying* to see things from another's point-of-view gives you an advantage every time. The person with one-way vision (their way) is only a "mere mortal," while one who uses "x-ray vision" to see through things from other viewpoints becomes Superman! What a deal — and it is all yours, free with a little effort.

Personality Characterized By This Color:

> **D** – **Green**: Like a "green light," they have "GO!" in their blood. Also, green as in "money," a powerful commodity to possess.

I – **Red**: Like the brightest color you can see, red is flashy. Everyone knows red stands out in the crowd.

S – **Blue**: Like the soft, stable color of the sky, it's gentle on the eyes, and stays the same no matter where you go in the world.

C – **Yellow**: Like a "caution light," they seem to say "Be careful! I would double-check that, if I were you!"

To understand how natural tendencies, or comfort zones, differ, think of this: When an "S" or a "C" is driving and sees the traffic signal turn yellow, he interprets it to mean "Stop!" To a "D" or an "I" it means "Gun it before you get stuck!"

Personality Most Like This Animal:

D – **Doberman**: They say this dog will bite your head off with little provocation. As long as he is fed and kept in a good environment, a Doberman seems pleasant enough. However, let something cross him or challenge his environment, and his true nature comes out. The Doberman functions best with a big challenge before him. He will keep burglars out of the house at all costs. His bark is almost as bad as his bite — you don't want to get in a fight with him! He doesn't like to lose. Remember Vince Lombardi? He was a classic high "D," who left us with this "D"-escriptive quote: "Winning isn't everything… it's the only thing!"

I – **Fluffy Puppy**: They like to play, and they find it difficult to get very serious about anything. They are most content when they are laughing and having fun. They want to appear "cute" in nature, loving strokes and pats at every opportunity. The high "I" functions best in response to praise or recognition. Speak kind words to them and their "tails" begin to wag. (Someone has said the reason dogs have so many friends is because they wag their tails and not their tongues!)

S – **Cat**: Cats move around the house at a leisurely pace, enjoying every corner. They find a certain few spots where they feel most comfortable and retreat there to relax. They like their own familiar territory. They like to be stroked and are wary of any surprises. They stay out of the way so no one will step on them. When someone jumps at them, they run away. They don't like conflict. They love to be appreciated and patted — they purr when you stroke them.

C – **Tropical Fish**: They swim to one side of their aquarium to check everything out; then to the other side to check everything out; then to the top to check everything out. They seem to enjoy making sure everything is okay in every area. They check each rock on the bottom of the tank. They swim over to check the ceramic figures. And then, they start their circuit all over again. They are curious in nature, and they function best when the environment is exactly to their liking. They don't like sudden change, but they do like to be fed and to maintain their constant state.

Personality Most Likely To Buy This Car:

D – **Mercedes** or **Cadillac**: This type appreciates a "power car" with status and prestige. If their budgets cannot afford luxury, they will still look for power.

I – **Convertible**: It doesn't matter what kind of car it is, as long as the roof goes down so the high "I" can wave at everyone. They like to see and be seen!

S – **Van** or **Station Wagon**: They want everyone to be comfortable and have their own space. Everyone needs a seat belt and enough cool air if it's warm outside.

C – **Toyota** or **Honda**: They look for an economical car receiving high marks from the consumer reviews. They want the most for their money.

Personality's Motto:

D – **"Go for it!"** You only go around once, so grab all the gusto you can get! The Nike advertisements sum it up best: "Just Do It!"

I – **"Lighten up!"** An "I" will not let things get intense. If things are getting serious, he will tell a joke. Life is too short to be miserable, so have a party. "Life is too mysterious... don't take it serious!"

S – **"One for all... all for one!"** Let's all pull together and we will do better! Many hands make light work. Let's row in the same direction. In short, they love the togetherness of a team.

C – **"If anything can go wrong, it will!"** Murphy's Law tells us the bad news — he must have been a "C." (It is not that they are negative or overly critical. It is just that they are so good at being right, it is easy for them to spot what is wrong. If you are a "C" type and this motto offends you, please forgive me. An alternative, more positive motto might be "Plan your work... then work your plan!" Remember, I am a High "I" and I want you to like me!)

Personality's Favorite Song:

D – **"I Did It My Way"** Nobody gave me what I have today. I worked hard. I know what it means to "pull myself up by my own boot straps." That's how they feel.

I – **"Celebration"** Everyone around the world, c'mon! We're gonna have a good time. Yeah!

S – **"Precious Memories"** or **"Will the Circle Be Unbroken?"** When will I see you again? I like you. I hate to say "good-bye." We will all be together in the sweet by-and-by.

C – **"The Gambler"** Know when to hold 'em... know when to fold 'em... know when to walk away... know when to run. To a "C" it's important to be right.

Personality's Philosophy

D – **"I want it yesterday!"** "Do you have a problem with that? If you don't like it — you can lump it! It's *your* job to learn to think like *me*. I don't have time to wait around for you to put me on your schedule. I need it now!"

I – **"Let the good times roll!"** "We don't have to find a party — we will take one with us wherever we go! Life was designed with me in mind."

S – **"Working together, we can do it!"** When Chrysler Corporation was almost broke, Lee Iacocca was hired to take over. The first thing he did was tell all the employees that they had a team project to complete. Without everyone working together, all would be lost. "But together, we can do it." Chrysler stock went from 50¢ in the early 1980s to $65.00 by the end of the decade, and the rest is history. Teamwork made the difference.

C – **"Don't show all your cards."** Be wise. Be careful. You don't have to tell everything you know. A fish would never get caught if he kept his mouth shut!

Personality's Favorite Magazine:

D – ***Money:*** All about prestige, fame, fortune, and those who have done it! "The proof is in the puddin'!"

I – ***People:*** Lots of pictures, little copy to read. The lengthiest stories are only a few paragraphs. For the most part, "I's" don't like to read. They like to look at pictures, to see "what's hot... and what's not!"

S – ***Us*** or ***Parents Magazine*** or ***The Reader's Digest:*** Close, warm, accommodating, these are relationship-oriented, neat and to-the-point. Many stories are so heartwarming they bring tears to your eyes.

C – ***Consumer Reports:*** "C" types want the greatest value for the dollar. They appreciate a good business deal, and they don't like being taken advantage of. They like to study their options before purchasing an item. They seldom buy on impulse because they want to know they are getting the best deal.

Personality's Target Practice Call:

D – **"Ready... Fire... Aim!"** High "D's" decide what they want to do... then they do it... then they check to see if it was the right thing to do or not.

I – **"Ready... Aim... Talk!"** High "I's" decide what they want to do... then check to see if it's the right thing to do or not... then talk about it. (Remember,

"I's" think talking about something and actually doing it are synonymous.)

S – **"Ready... Ready... Ready..."** High "S's" try to decide what to do, and then they try deciding to decide what to do. And they don't want to offend anyone in the process.

C – **"Ready... Aim... Aim... Aim..."** High "C's" decide what to do, but once they settle on a course of action, they check, double-check and triple-check their plan. Then they worry whether or not it will work.

Personality's Greatest Need:

D – **Challenge**. Give me the opportunity to spread my wings and fly!

I – **Recognition**. Call my name, let me stand up and be seen. Notice me and I will follow you anywhere!

S – **Appreciation**. Make me feel like I pleased you and did a good job. Don't recognize me publicly too much. I embarrass easily.

C – **Quality answers**. Not *just* any answers, but good, solid, substantial answers. It is vitally important to be correct, so do your research and know that you know what you know.

Review

Suppose you are working on a project with a group of people. If you are able to apply your understanding of the basic needs and thought patterns of the four personality types, you will be "light years" ahead in the progress of your work.

Remember, the "D" thinks in terms of *"What?" What* is

going on here? *What* is the bottom line? *What* are we trying to accomplish? *What* is the agenda? He is motivated by his basic needs of challenge (*what* is the obstacle?) and control (*what* can I do?). He wants a piece of the action. Give him some control and it will challenge him. He likes choices — conflicts do not bother him. He sees them both as part of the territory. Remember his thought patterns of "what" and the need for "challenge" and "control," and you will be speaking his language.

The "I" thinks in terms of *"Who?" Who* is going? *Who* will be there? *Who* will I see? *Who* will I know? He is motivated by his basic needs of recognition (*who* will recognize me?) and social interaction (*who* can make this fun?). He stands out in a crowd. It is impossible to give him too much attention. Remember the thought pattern of "who" and the basic needs of "recognition" and social "interaction," and you will be speaking his language.

The "S" thinks in terms of *"How?" How* do you want this job done? *How* do you want me to do it? *How* do you want it to look? *How* will I know if I have done it right? He is motivated by his basic needs of appreciation (*how* can I gain your approval?) and service (*how* am I doing?). He wants to feel that he has pleased you. Nothing makes him feel better than knowing he did as you expected and everything went according to schedule and plan. If *you* are pleased with the way things turned out, he is *more* pleased. Remember the thought pattern of "how" and the basic needs of "appreciation" and "desire to please," and you will be speaking his language.

The "C" thinks in terms of *"Why?" Why* are we doing this? *Why* are we working on this job? *Why* was I assigned this task? *Why* am I reading this book? He is motivated by his basic needs of quality answers (*why* is this happening?) and correctness (*why* are we doing it this way?). It is better to tell a "C" you don't know an answer than to fake it. Better yet, tell him you don't know but will do a little research and get back to him later when you find a satisfactory answer. Then, do your homework. Such a "C" will respect you, admire your diligence, and help you complete your task in style. Remember the thought pattern of "why" and the basic needs of "quality answers" and "correctness," and you will be speaking his language.

Personality Capsule Focus:

TYPE	THOUGHT PATTERN	BASIC NEED	IDENTIFIER
D	*What?*	Control	**D**ominance
I	*Who?*	Recognition	**I**nteraction
S	*How?*	Appreciation	**S**upport
C	*Why?*	Quality Answers	**C**orrectness

(See the "Personality Chart" on the next page for an overview of the themes presented in this chapter.)

	D WHAT?	**I** WHO?	**S** HOW?	**C** WHY?
Question:	WHAT?	WHO?	HOW?	WHY?
Color:	Green	Red	Blue	Yellow
Animal:	Doberman	Fluffy Puppy	Cat	Tropical Fish
Car:	Mercedes Cadillac	Convertible	Van Station Wagon	Toyota Honda
Motto:	"Go for it!"	"Lighten up!"	"All for one... one for all!"	"If something can go wrong, it will!"
Song:	"I Did It My Way"	"Celebration"	"Precious Memories" "Will the Circle Be Unbroken"	"The Gambler"
Philosophy:	"I want it yesterday!"	"Let the good times roll!"	"Working together, we can do it!"	"Don't show all your cards!"
Magazine:	*Money*	*People*	*Us* or *Parents Magazine* or *Reader's Digest*	*Consumer Reports*
Target:	"Ready... Fire... Aim!"	"Ready... Aim... Talk!"	"Ready... Ready... Ready..."	"Ready... Aim... Aim...Aim..."
Need:	Challenge Dominance	Recognition Interaction	Appreciation Service	Quality Answers Correctness

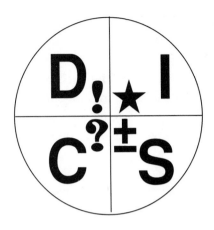

Chapter Seven:

Reading People – Overview

I first met Dr. Frank Wichern, psychologist, when I was enrolled as a graduate student at Dallas Theological Seminary. I had been in school for about two weeks and had to go for my first-year interview. Before entering seminary, each student was required to take the MMPI (Minnesota Multiphasic Personality Inventory). This testing instrument distinguishes between normal, neurotic, and psychotic personality characteristics. It also has industrial, counseling, and marital applications, as a predictor of specialized interests.

I walked into Dr. Wichern's office and sat down. He opened my folder and reviewed my test results. He looked at me, smiled and said, "Well, I have some good news for you and I have some bad news." I said, "Tell me the good news first."

He continued, "Well, you are a real 'people person.' You are going to do really well in life because you like people so much. They will be drawn to you!" I said, "Great! What's the bad news?" He said, "Well, the bad news is this — people with your personality profile never finish graduate school! They can't sit still long enough to make it through the process."

I was amazed. I had only been in graduate school two weeks, and already I had thought about dropping out. How did he know that about me? We had met only five minutes before. He proceeded to tell me how I felt about life and "things" in general. He *read me* like a book!

Although I cannot explain it, something happened to me that day. Something "clicked" in my mind. Most of my life, I had fought with myself over my own personality, temperament, tendencies and feelings. I couldn't understand why I always felt so active and outgoing. I tried to make myself more reserved. I tried my best to be quiet and withdrawn. I thought by doing so, I would be a better Christian. I thought being a good Christian meant becoming the *opposite* of how I really felt. If I could just get sad and depressed, then I could be like most Christians I knew! My attempts only frustrated me. I felt as if I was living a lie.

When I finally began to learn these truths concerning personalities, I discovered (at long last!) that God had made me a certain way. He gifted me and made me to be outgoing and people-oriented. His primary goal was not to "un-gift" or "un-make" me, but to *control* me. Change would come as a by-product of His control. I could actually *enjoy* being myself—what a freeing truth!

I, too, wanted to read and understand people in a way I never had before. I wanted to help others discover how life and relationships work. In time, I began to understand the principles related in this book — some of the most valuable information I possess as a human being! I will always be grateful to Dr. Wichern for that initial visit in his office years ago.

The following overviews are drawn from notes Dr. Wichern put together. I have modified a few points for further emphasis and clarity. As you read them, keep in mind that hardly anyone is "purely" a "D," or an "I," or an "S," or a "C." Research indicates that 80% of the general population has at least two traits as primary factors in their personality makeup. (More will be presented about this in Chapter 8, "Why Opposites Attract.") All of us are composites of D–I–S–C, to a greater or lesser degree.

HIGH "D"

BASIC MOTIVATION:
- Challenge
- Choices
- Control

ENVIRONMENT NEEDS:
- Freedom
- Authority
- Varied activities
- Difficult assignments
- Opportunity for advancement

RESPONDS BEST TO A LEADER WHO:
- Provides direct answers
- Sticks to business
- Stresses goals
- Provides pressure
- Allows freedom for personal accomplishment

NEEDS TO LEARN THAT:
- People are important
- Relaxation is not a crime
- Some controls are necessary
- Everyone has a boss
- Verbalizing conclusions helps others understand them better

HIGH "I"

BASIC MOTIVATION:
- Recognition
- Approval
- Popularity

ENVIRONMENT NEEDS:
- Prestige
- Friendly relationships
- Opportunities to influence others
- Opportunities to inspire others
- Chance to verbalize ideas

RESPONDS BEST TO A LEADER WHO:
- Is a democratic leader and friend
- Provides social involvement outside of work
- Provides recognition of abilities
- Offers incentives for risk-taking
- Creates an atmosphere of excitement

NEEDS TO LEARN THAT:
- Time must be managed
- Too much optimism can be harmful
- Listening is important
- Tasks must be completed
- Accountability is imperative

HIGH "S"

BASIC MOTIVATION:
- Security
- Appreciation
- Assurance

ENVIRONMENT NEEDS:
- An area of specialization
- Identification with a group
- Established work pattern
- Stability of situation
- Consistent, familiar environment

RESPONDS BEST TO A LEADER WHO:
- Is relaxed and amiable
- Allows time to adjust to change in plans
- Serves as a friend
- Allows people to work at their own pace
- Clearly defines goals and means of reaching them

NEEDS TO LEARN THAT:
- Change provides opportunity
- Friendship isn't everything
- Discipline is good
- It is all right to say, "No!"
- Being a "servant" does not mean being a "sucker"

HIGH "C"

BASIC MOTIVATION:
- Quality answers
- Excellence
- Value

ENVIRONMENT NEEDS:
- Clearly-defined tasks and explanations
- Sufficient time and resources to accomplish tasks
- Team participation
- Limited risks
- Assignments that require planning and precision

RESPONDS BEST TO A LEADER WHO:
- Provides reassurance
- Maintains a supportive atmosphere
- Provides an open-door policy
- Defines concise operating standards
- Is detail-oriented

NEEDS TO LEARN THAT:
- Total support is not always necessary
- Thorough explanation is not always possible
- Deadlines must be met
- Taking a calculated risk can be profitable
- There are varying degrees of excellence

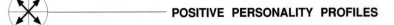

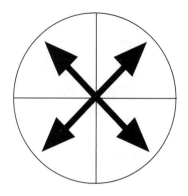

Chapter Eight:

Why Opposites Attract

The ancient Greeks had a powerful idea, presented in the form of a myth. They said that in order to render humankind less powerful, the gods split him in two and made male and female. As a result, our lives have become one long search for our missing "other half." But when we do find our "other half," most of us set about the ironic and frustrating task of remaking that mate into an image of ourselves. As experience proves, the effort is futile! Without a blending of personalities, through efforts to communicate and understand each other, one mate's personality will find expression at the expense of the other's. Then the more probable question becomes: which of *us* will our *marriage* most likely come to resemble?

This is particularly odd, since we usually are initially attracted to someone who is different from ourselves because we enjoy the "freshness" of a new and different personality style.

It is important to keep in mind our Model of Human Behavior on page 20. You may wish to turn back and quickly get a mental image in your mind. As we examine the model, we can observe the similarities and differences of each personality type:

Notice that "D's" and "S's" are opposites, and that "I's" and "C's" are opposites. All other combinations have at least one trait in common:

D / I –   task-oriented and *outgoing* (D)
          people-oriented and *outgoing* (I)
D / C –   *task-oriented* and outgoing (D)
          task-oriented and reserved (C)
D / S –   true opposites – little common ground

I / D –   people-oriented and *outgoing* (I)
          task-oriented and *outgoing* (D)
I / S –   *people-oriented* and outgoing (I)
          people-oriented and reserved (S)
I / C –   true opposites – little common ground

S / C –   people-oriented and *reserved* (S)
          task-oriented and *reserved* (C)
S / I –   *people-oriented* and reserved (S)
          people-oriented and outgoing (I)
S / D –   true opposites – little common ground

C / S –   task-oriented and *reserved* (C)
          people-oriented and *reserved* (S)
C / D –   *task-oriented* and reserved (C)
          task-oriented and outgoing (D)
C / I –   true opposites – little common ground

As clearly shown, the most opposite types are "D's" and "S's"; and "I's" and "C's." So, why do opposites attract?

"D's" usually gravitate toward "S's" because "D's" like to lead, while "S's" like to follow. "S's" find "D's" because "S's" sometimes feel insecure while "D's" seem to radiate confidence.

"I's" usually gravitate toward "C's" because "C's" know how to think things through *systematically* and logically, while "I's" like *spontaneous* fun. "C's" find "I's" because "C's" are more serious but are trying to lighten up their lives a little.

Of course, these are not the only opposite traits that exist. Notice in the previous listing how combinations of characteristics interact and differ. Some are outgoing, others are reserved. Some are task-oriented, others are people-oriented. Most people, whether or not they realize it, are attracted to someone who can "complete their half," or "cover" for their areas of weakness.

A "D" who is a risk-taking, **driving, demanding, doer** can be attracted to a "C" because of a **cautious, calculating** style. An "I" who can **influence** and **impress** others can be attracted to an "S" because of a **sweet, soft, steady, stable** style.

Because we are all blends of D–I–S–C to a greater or lesser degree, we can compliment each other's strengths and weaknesses. Our unique combination allows us ability to "balance out" when interacting with others. (The problem comes when we focus on each other's weaknesses instead of strengths.)

Personally, I am a high "I / S" combination. Thus, my people skills are stronger than my task-orientation. Because I am aware of this, I realize I must focus more clearly on tasks (i.e., "getting the job done"), rather than interacting with people (which always comes naturally — I love this part of my life!). There has never been a morning when I have looked in the mirror and said, "Remember to speak to everyone you see today, and be friendly, too!" All that happens naturally, because it is part of my personality style. Rather, I have to remind myself each morning: "Don't forget to go to work! Be sure to complete your necessary assignments and tasks. Plan your work, and then work your plan!"

A "D / C" combination would be just the opposite. Task skills come naturally to these types. However, they must concentrate on people skills or go through the day ignoring everyone. When you pass them, they seem cold, distant and aloof. Actually, they are preoccupied with their tasks.

The "D / C" type is task-oriented, while an "I / S" is primarily interested in people. The "D / C" type works well on planning committees. The "I / S" type works well on welcoming committees. The "D / C" often lacks people skills, while the "I / S" needs to become more task-oriented. "D / C" types and "I / S" types often clash when they begin working together. They are attracted to each other because of their differences — and that is good — but those differences can become repellant — and that is bad. While the "D / C" focuses on getting the job done, the "I / S" concentrates on building up people and developing better relationships. Do you see what happens? They really need each other for balance — but it is more difficult to see a need if you don't want to see it *or if you have not been trained to recognize it*. (Thus the need for reading this book!)

The "D / I" combination (**dominant** and **inspirational**) is *outgoing* — and is both task- and people-oriented. They are easily attracted to an "S / C" type (**supportive** and **cautious**), who is *reserved* but also is both task- and people-oriented.

I am often amazed by how numerous churches govern themselves. They elect from their congregations high-powered, successful, driving business leaders, expecting them to come together and cooperate as a group. These people did not get where they are in life by working in a group! So, rather than helping their church, they usually split it! A better leadership team would be made up of some "D's," some "I's," some "S's," and some "C's," who would look at issues from all points of view and make decisions benefiting everyone.

The most difficult combinations occur when people have a "D / S" or an "I / C" blend within themselves. They are a walking contradiction in terms! (Remember earlier I noted that the "D / S" and "I / C" personality combinations were the most unusual to occur. Although unusual, they certainly are not impossible.) It does not occur often, but such a people can be extremely confused inside, until they gain understanding of themselves. A "D / S" person wants to be in charge (**dominant**), but also really enjoys helping (**supportive**). When in charge, they are frustrated when no one else helps. When helping, they are frustrated when no one is in charge!

The "I / C" person really loves people (**inspirational**), but knows how important it is to research the facts and to do a job correctly (**cautious**). When they are having fun, they feel guilty for not studying. When they are studying, the feel guilty for wishing they could be with people having fun.

Technically, these are not "split personalities." These are

simply people who have a blend that is more difficult for them to understand. Interpreting their temperament's conflicting signals causes them (and their friends) a little more frustration at times. I have counseled several of these type individuals. Perhaps more than any other combination, they sense a spirit of relief when they finally see what is going on inside themselves. As a result, their inner conflicts find resolution.

A "D / S" combination is unique, in that it is both outgoing and task-oriented at times, while reserved and people-oriented at other times. These people are both tough and gentle. Think of a nurse's vocation, requiring toughness and gentleness. Not always an easy job!

An "I / C" combination is unique, in that it is both outgoing and people-oriented at times, while reserved and task-oriented at other times. These types can be the life of the party and also the hardest worker in the office when completing a project. Think of a really good salesperson, warm and friendly, able to make you feel good, while also handling details in completing the sale.

Again, the "D / S" or "I / C" combinations are fairly uncommon, but they do exist. Usually, someone who is *primarily* a "D" is *secondarily* an "I" or a "C." And someone who is *primarily* an "I" may *secondarily* be an "S" or a "D." Likewise, one who is *primarily* an "S" might *secondarily* be a "C" or an "I." And someone who is *primarily* a "C" usually is *secondarily* an "S" or a "D." Refer to the Model of Human Behavior "pie" in Chapter One and you can see how this flows.

Personally, I believe it is better to look at your *two primary characteristics* to see a more accurate and enlightening picture of yourself, rather than simply focusing on one trait. As mentioned previously, 80% of the general population has two traits which are primary in their personality style. Again, this is referred to as your unique "blend." My "I" and my "S" are above the midline, and my "D" and my "C" are both below the midline on my personality profile. As I see it in my mind, I know I must constantly work to *lower* my "I" and my "S" (not socialize too much), and *raise* my "D" and my "C" (to accomplish tasks).

When I finally grasped this dynamic concept, I was able to understand myself more fully for the first time. Most of my adult life, I was secretly frustrated and disappointed for feeling the way I did. I tried everything I knew to become the *opposite* of how I felt inside. But nothing worked. Now, rather than concentrating on *changing* who I am, I can focus on *controlling* my behavior. I can still love people while getting my work done! I am learning to work *with* myself, rather than *against* myself. Sadly, many people have told me they have become their own worst enemies, defeating themselves because they have lacked understanding about the special way God has made them. Hopefully, this information will open your eyes to becoming the fulfilled, balanced person God designed you to be!

Help is available when you identify and understand your own unique personality style. When you recognize your strengths and grow in your weaknesses, you profit immensely. After all, as noted elsewhere, relationships are our greatest source of joy and yet, are our greatest source of pain. No one on his death bed ever said, "I only wish I had spent a little more time at the office." Life is too short and relationships are too dear to miss the real thing. I trust you will learn to utilize these insights on a daily basis. You will be the one who wins. It is really true that "having the right tools is 95% of a job well done."

If you would like to receive a complete profile assessment and "D-I-S-Cover" exactly what your unique combination is, along with the type-blend pattern you possess, you may order a variety of assessment instruments from Personality Insights. Descriptions of several and ordering information are in the back of this book.

I have completed profiles on all of my children and spouse, and using the information, I try to treat each one differently, according to her unique personality.

Three *self-scoring* profiles are available: *1.)* a child's instrument, for Kindergarten through Elementary School, called *All About BOTS, All About You; 2.)* a profile for teenagers, called *Get Real! Who You Are and Why You Do Those Things;* and *3.)* an adult profile, known as the *Personality Insights Profile Assessment.* By "self-scoring" we mean that the entire process can be completed by yourself, and information on all the styles is included in booklet form, to help you understand the meaning of your own, unique personality profile.

A fourth type of profile is available, as well — an in-depth, *computer-scored* profile for adults, featuring a detailed evaluation report complete with graphs and specific information on your own unique behavioral style, created especially for you. It is explained in detail in the Personality Insights product catalog, available upon request.

Again, see the last pages of this book for more information.

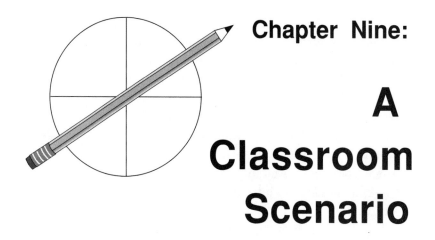

Chapter Nine:

A Classroom Scenario

Now let's take a look at personality types "at work" in a classroom setting:

The teacher stands up, ready to begin her lesson. Because she is unaware of the different personality types, she is already at a disadvantage. She asks, "Boys and girls, who discovered America?" Rocky, the high "D," bursts out, "Columbus!" The teacher frowns: "Rocky, you didn't even raise your hand!" He replies, "You asked a question — I thought you wanted an answer!" The teacher is blown away.

Again the teacher asks, "All right, boys and girls, who discovered America?" Sparky, the high "I," shoots his hand up and down, waving his arm side to side. She sighs: "Okay, Sparky, who discovered America?" He replies, "Could you give me a hint?" The teacher thinks to herself, "How could the child raise his hand and not know the answer?" Their problem lies in the perception: she asked, "Who discovered America?", but Sparky heard, "Would anyone like to talk?" *That's exactly what he heard!*

The teacher strolls over to Suzie's desk. She has to call on Suzie, the high "S," because Suzie never raises her hand. The teacher asks, "Suzie, who discovered America?" And Suzie replies, "Well, in reading over this material and doing my homework last night, it seems — I may be wrong and I don't want to offend anyone, and if anyone wants to disagree with me that's okay, or if someone wants to take my turn I'll let them because I have probably already taken too long — but I think... was it Columbus?" And the teacher wonders to herself, "Why is this child so shy and intimidated?"

Then the teacher quizzes Claire, the high "C." And Claire responds: "Who discovered America... I'm not sure I understand the question. Are you wanting me to say Columbus? Before Columbus came, the Indians were here, and before the Indians, the Vikings. So, I'm not sure I understand the question."

About this time, Rocky yells, "Stop it, Claire! You're driving us crazy — you're driving us all nuts! You just keep doing this over and over!" Sparky says, "A fight! A fight's breaking out! Wow — this is exciting!" Suzie softly says, "It's all my fault. It was me. I caused this!" The teacher is at a total loss... and very frustrated.

If the teacher understood personality interaction, when Rocky shouted out "Columbus!" she could have said, "Right, Rocky. That's good. I'm glad you knew the answer..." (She would have *expected* him to blurt it out.) "Rocky, I'm glad you're in my class. You're going to grow up to be president of the student body, or captain of the football team. You may even grow up to be my pastor! Rocky, the key to your life is self-control, and I am here to help you develop it. Next time, raise your hand. You got the answer — that's good." She would be able to train him according to his personality. His *challenge* would be to raise his hand, but his *confirmation* would be that he knew the right answer.

Likewise, when Sparky asked, "Could you give me a hint?", she would have been ready, recognizing him as a high "I" who loves to talk. Even though wondering if he is "brain dead" to raise his hand without knowing the answer, she would have been ready to help him. She might have hinted: "Col... Col... Col... um... um — say, is that a *bus* going by outside?" And Sparky would have blurted, "Columbus! Gee, I didn't even know I knew it!" She and he would be excited, and she would have given him some *recognition.*

She could have asked Suzie softly, "Who discovered America? You don't have to go into a lot of detail — just tell me quickly and I will tell the rest of the class." Suzie would have responded, "Well, was it Columbus?" And the teacher could have said, "That's right! Class, did you hear that? Suzie said 'Columbus,' which is the right answer." This would take the pressure off Suzie, helping her not to feel too self-conscious. Then, in a quiet moment, she could say to Suzie, "I appreciate you so much. You do your homework and try really hard. I know you can 'get lost' in our class sometimes because there are so many people in here, but I am so glad you are in my class...!" Do you hear and feel all that *appreciation, acceptance* and *love?* Suzie needs that like flowers need sunshine — in order to "blossom."

Obviously, Claire has a need to be correct. That is why she covered every possibility with Columbus, the Indians and the Vikings. In response, the teacher could have replied, "I'm so glad you're a thinker. You are probably going to grow up to be a doctor or a lawyer or a scientist. But just for right now, bottom line, who discovered America?" And Claire would have replied, "Columbus."

When the teacher creates a climate for learning by understanding personality types, everyone in the classroom can begin to learn in harmony, and everything works together. The teacher understands and teaches the most important lesson in her classroom; namely, that each student is different… which is perfectly normal. Rather than being continually "ambushed," she learns to "head 'em off at the pass!" (Remember the old Cowboys 'n Indians routine?)

Each child responds according to his *predictable pattern* of behavior. When these patterns are known and recognized in advance, teachers (and parents) can work in better harmony with children, rather than creating power struggles. Truly, they can create "win–win" situations.

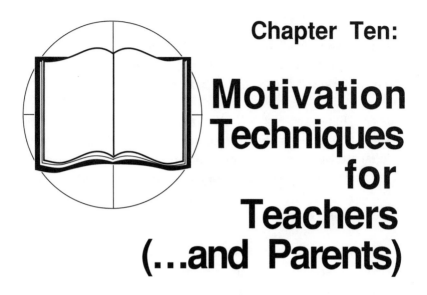

Chapter Ten:

Motivation Techniques for Teachers (...and Parents)

"How can I motivate my students?" This question is asked often. Well, in one sense, children are *already* motivated — to do exactly what *they* want to do! Unfortunately, what they want to do is seldom what you want them to do.

In this chapter, we will look at some techniques you can use to *create a different climate* in the classroom, helping the students under your care to "get on track." For the most part, people do things for their own reasons. (Even a submissive "S" personality strives to please for his own reasons: doing so reinforces his "comfort zone.") If you can *engineer an environment* which causes people to *want to respond* in a better way, you will create a "win–win" situation.

For example, if a mother wants her son to get out of bed in the morning when he doesn't want to, she may have difficulty doing so without an argument or conflict. But if the house were on fire and she awakened him to say, "Son, I think you ought to know... your closet has just burned down!", he would discover his own "instant motivation" to hop from between the sheets. The difference? Just a change in the environment!

This chapter is devoted to explaining how to work with your environment—how to *create a climate* which puts students in a better position to mature, and encourages them to become the responsible individuals they were meant to be.

Motivation Techniques for "D's"

The "D" type needs a challenge, along with some control. In the classroom or at home, you need to give them opportunities to lead. Assign them a chapter or a study unit to teach to the other students, under your supervision. They will rise to the occasion. They will also respect you more for giving them room to grow—that's what they want and need. They are bottom line people, thinking in terms of "what?". Let them be a part of the action by making things happen.

The best "discipleship" model is found in apprenticeship. Years ago, young people worked beside skilled craftsmen while learning their trade. As a teacher, you need to use this tried and proven "mentoring" technique. (The goal is a little different however — your students may not have the goal of becoming teachers. Your goal is to model "balanced humanness" for them.) A "D" grows up to be a leader, positive or negative, and you can help him sharpen his leadership skills in a positive manner.

When working with "D" type students, remember that they not only need room to grow, but also need room to fail. They probably will do a better job in *taking on* the project than in ultimately *completing* it. Give them crystal clear boundaries — preferably written down — so they can understand exactly what is expected. As they sense "ownership" of the project (control), they will become self-motivated, working with you, rather than creating disharmony. "D" types are full of nervous energy. Something is going on all the time, either inwardly or outwardly. When they "own a piece of the rock," they will be a help to you, rather than a hindrance.

"D's" need you to be consistent and fair with them as much as possible. They feel cheated when the rules change in the middle of the game. As a teacher or parent, let them know they have a right to verbalize their feelings to you in a polite manner. Tell them that as long as they respond with respect, rather than react in anger, you will listen to them.

Consider our "D" type teaching the chapter scenario suggested earlier. This will require you to expend a little extra time and energy up front, but it will prove worthwhile in the long run. The "D" student will respond to the challenge and will probably do a great job. And he will save you the energy of teaching the unit yourself! As a side benefit, you will create a better environment — with students learning from other students (often fostering healthy competition) rather than always learning from the teacher (an authority figure). Be on your guard though — your "D" may even do a better job than you!

Bring some closure to this project by giving the student your "professional" evaluation. Share your encouragements publicly in front of the class, and share your "suggestions" for improvement one-on-one. ("Praise publicly... reprove privately.") Let him have other opportunities to lead or teach again, often. Remember, the concept is to create a climate or environment where the "D" feels you are on his team, rather than on his back! He will be your most loyal supporter and will help solve your classroom's behavior problems.

Motivation Techniques for "I's"

The "I" types need recognition, so give them some! They love to have fun in school... and wherever they go. They are often labeled as "class clowns." You can avoid their disruptions by tapping into their desire to be "onstage," up in front of everyone, as outgoing, energetic leaders.

Ask high "I" students to help you invent a new game for the class. They love an opportunity to try new things. Give them a chapter or a unit in a particular area (i.e., history, English, math, science, etc.) and ask them to create a game for the class to play. They may want to use a game already in existence (like "Jeopardy!" or "Trivial Pursuit"), or they may create something entirely new. Give them enough freedom to succeed — or fail. The result will be a great learning experience for them, as well as for the rest of the class. (By the way, the people who invented "Trivial Pursuit" made millions of dollars on what is basically an educational game. Who knows — perhaps you have a little gold mine already sitting there in your class!)

Remember, "I's" think in terms of "who?" They will want lots of people involved in their project, including themselves. As a child, my favorite weekly activity was the Friday afternoon spelling bee. Although I did not understand myself at the time, I look back now and see what was taking place: I got to stand up *publicly,* spell *out loud,* and had an environment to *win* the contest and get some *recognition.* No wonder I liked it! That environment motivated me to study my spelling words every week. I am still an excellent speller today, thanks to some smart teachers who gave me the opportunity to participate in a game.

High "I" children need a stern hand, offering specific guidelines. Again, as with the "D" child, write (contract) everything down, eliminating possibilities for misunderstanding. The clearer the guidelines and achievement goals, the better off everyone will be.

Give a lot of encouragement, as well as deadlines, along the way. For instance, if the game-lesson session is assigned on Monday, to be taught on Friday, check every day during the week for an update. Otherwise, the plan is sure to fail. They will put it off until the last minute, then find the project impossible to accomplish.

You must communicate this message to these students: "I believe in you!" If you do, they will rise to the occasion. If they happen to fail for any reason, quickly give them opportunity to try again. "I" types hate to fail at anything because they feel you no longer like them. Don't substantiate their feelings by "writing them off," or not giving them other chances when they fail.

Finally, "I" children need freedom to verbalize their ideas without worrying about personal attacks. Often, their schemes, ideas, plans and projects are full of hot air. But just as often, they simply need time to develop, to gel, to solidify. Let them know, "I'm on your side. I am for you!" Then, "I's" will blossom like roses. Most high "I's" are better talkers than they are thinkers. And they certainly are better "talkers" than "doers." Let them develop a way to verbalize educational skills by means of games and outward activities. Your other students will learn a lot — and have fun in the process.

Motivation Techniques for "S's"

The "S" type student needs appreciation. He needs to know that he is doing what you expect of him. He doesn't like surprises or being put on the spot. More than likely, he will not want to be put up on the stage or in front of the class. You can help him best by allowing him to help you.

"S" types feel stability is important. Although they may not come right out and say it, they are thinking, "Please hold my hand. Don't run ahead of me. I want to know where you are, so please help me."

They love to please. They think in terms of "how" you want this done. Therefore, their most motivating environment is simply allowing them to be your assistants. I was administering the Child's Personality Profile to a class of students one day, and an "S" type child was petrified. Being in uncertain waters, he was very much afraid. I spent extra time with him and told him he was my "assistant." I let him help me take up pencils, pass out booklets, etc. That night at the parents' meeting, his mother told me how much I had helped him. When he came home from school, he had told her, "Mama, when I grow up, I want to be an *assistant!*" He needed a little extra assurance and affection in a stabilized environment — something familiar in unfamiliar territory.

"S's" need to work at their own pace. They do better when they are not rushed, in an environment of "peace," rather than conflict. They want as little conflict as possible. And they need their own space, allowing them to function within their boundaries. If you let them grade papers or record information in your grade book, let them know how long they have and exactly what you expect of them.

One last word: Probably more than any of your other students, "S" types will be the ones you must seek out. They are not pushy, but they do have a secret longing to be useful and helpful. As their teacher or parent, you can enhance their lives by providing them with opportunities to help you — while also developing their abilities and self-esteem.

Motivation Techniques for "C's"

The "C" type student needs quality answers. He is curious and always wondering or asking "why?". You can help such a student to excel by putting him in an environment with freedom to explore the unknown. Assign an area to investigate, with a report back to the class. Present it as an "Adventure in Research," and "C" students will take off with it. To them, research *is* adventure!

Their minds are often filled with unanswered questions, many of which will "bug the daylights out of you!" I have a list of unanswerable questions "C's" have asked me over the years: "Since Adam was the first person created, did he have a navel?" "Did the first trees God made have rings inside them?" "If everything is perfect in heaven and there is no evil there, how will we know it's good — with nothing bad to compare it to?" All good questions... all of which I cannot answer!

"C" types need freedom to ask their questions without fearing they will be laughed at or made fun of. Whether their questions are good or bad is not the issue. They simply must feel free to ask them.

When you give them a "research adventure" assignment, make sure your instructions are clear. You may even need to repeat them several times. More than likely, your "C" student will do more than you have asked. Keep in mind that "C's" have a problem with deadlines, because they want to keep gathering additional data. They always feel they could do better if they could go over their project *one more time.*

They will do quality work for you. So, be sure to give them extra credit for their work. They won't need it, usually, because they will already have a good grade. But the additional credit "balances their ledger," and it helps to give them encouragement and show "extra" appreciation.

Remember, "C's" don't handle criticism well. They have a strong desire to be correct in all their work. If you find them in error, say to them, "This is excellent work. You may need to double-check this one area (pointing to their error)." It is better to *gently redirect* them to the proper information or answers they seek than to tell them bluntly they are wrong — they do not handle criticism very well. However, if it is "their idea," they will be glad they thought of it! Allow them to verbalize their findings to the class. This technique will help other students see the value and fun in learning on their own.

Summary

Each child is unique. There is absolutely no method for motivating every one the same way. However, by looking at projects through the filter and perspective of different personality types, your chances for success rise dramatically. Please note, there is a big difference between *motivating* someone by genuinely helping them to develop their God-given abilities versus *manipulating* them into doing what you want them to do for your own personal, selfish reasons. The former focuses on helping the individual, whereas the latter focuses on satisfying yourself.

Even if it "goes against the grain" of your own personality type, accept this personal challenge to expand your own vision — from simply seeing and doing things the ways you have *always* seen and done them — to creating exciting, motivational environments for your students' growth and learning. You can lead them into the future through creative, innovative, insightful applications of these personality principles.

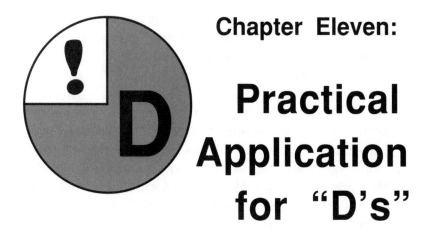

Chapter Eleven:

Practical Application for "D's"

"D's" must develop the skills required to become team players. They have strong desires to "take charge," which in turn tempt them to "fly solo." Although "D's" may be able to do some things better by themselves, they can have more influence as members of a team. Also they are more healthy emotionally when they know how to interact and cooperate with others.

"D's" should train themselves consciously to bring others into their decision-making processes. To succeed in leadership, they must become aware of the needs and drives of others. Working with "D's" who refuse to "play second fiddle" can be exasperating. Oftentimes, they display this attitude unknowingly because they do not understand their own emotions and actions. Using a positive approach in explaining to "D's" why they have such dominant drives and determination can be helpful to them.

Choices, Not Commands

Because "D's" don't like being told what to do, it is

important to give them choices. Instead of telling a "D" child that he *must* go to bed at nine o'clock, tell him he must *choose* between going to bed at eight-thirty or nine o'clock. Ask, "Which time do you choose?"

Explain that you as the parent have the responsibility to try to give guidance to the child. Express the attitude of a loving leader, fun but fair. Teach "D's" responsibility by allowing them to make some decisions for themselves. Make sure they realize there are consequences if they choose not to act responsibly. Get "D" children to agree beforehand on the discipline they will receive if they violate the rules.

Learn to ask questions rather than making dogmatic statements: "How much time do you think you need to spend on your homework?" is a lot better than "You must spend at least one hour on your homework." Usually (and oddly enough, I must add), the child will choose a greater amount of time than you would have required. When they say, "Two hours," just smile, hug them and say, "One hour will be fine, but you use the necessary time you need." Face it, sooner or later your children will be grown, and the sooner they become responsible for their own actions, the better. Remember... *questions,* rather than dogmatic statements. Try it!

Do not let "D's" control you. They need parameters for their behaviors and actions. They will always stretch the limits; you must let them know how far is too far. Draw your "action line" before pressed to your "anger line." Then you will be enforcing limits, rather than reacting irrationally. Children will learn to respond to *limits,* rather than to *threats.* "D's" desperately need good role models for self-control. Show "D's" how to stay in control of their emotions by remaining calm.

Meekness Is Not Weakness

"D's" should be taught that demonstrating meekness is not showing weakness. Jesus, the most powerful man who ever lived, was meek. Meekness is actually "power under control." The harder it is to stay under control, the more powerful meekness becomes.

Following the crowd and being like everyone else requires no personal power or strength. It takes real power to be different and to do what is right. Anyone can "blow his top." Those who are truly meek are able to control their feelings and actions. "D's" who struggle with anger should literally walk away from an explosive situation. They should not do what comes naturally to them, or what they feel like doing at the moment. Chances are, that is the worst thing a "D" could do!

Do not push "D's." They tend to respond like wild animals that have been cornered — they attack! Give "D's" a way out, by giving them a choice or negotiating a settlement which allows them to save face rather than feeling intimidated.

Be Under Authority

"D's" must learn to respect authority figures in their lives, such as the police, teachers, and bosses — even when these people seem to make life difficult for them.

"D's" do not enjoy being submissive. Something inside them cries for independence and yearns for freedom. However, the most tormenting bondage they can experience is enslavement to their own personality's emotions and actions. True freedom comes through submission to authority rather than fighting against it.

We cannot truly *possess* authority until we learn to *submit* to it. This is a basic truth of all military discipline: You can't *be* in authority until you learn to be *under* authority. The most powerful people in the world still operate under some type of authority. Once we learn to work in *dependence* upon others, and not *independence* of them, we will be more successful.

When "D's" respond poorly, they actually lose authority, because they put themselves in a position for others to no longer respect them. They surrender power, control, and influence. While many "D's" will not initially view submission as weak or cowardly, submitting to authority will still provide them tremendous opportunity to learn how "strength under control" really operates. Understanding the principle of respect for authority is imperative for "D's".

Showing Feelings

"D's" also need to learn how to show their emotions without "blowing their tops." Their short fuses get them into trouble. When faced with opposition, one must choose between *responding* and *reacting* — there is a big difference! *Responding* is using awareness of the needs and feelings of others to phrase what you need to say. *Reacting* is saying whatever comes off the top of your head, regardless of how it affects others. *Responding* is like defusing dynamite, while *reacting* is like lighting a match to it. When we respond, rather than react, we remain in control. Learning to respond properly is perhaps the greatest challenge for a "D."

A "D's" attitude about strength may cause him to see crying as a sign of weakness. On the other hand, expressing his feelings — allowing himself to be transparent with others — can sometimes be very helpful... and powerful.

Crushed Through Crisis

An obstacle most "D's" face is that they have not been *broken.* They are so full of themselves that they can lose effectiveness in identifying with and helping meet the needs of others. The "D" type thinks everyone should be like him! They want to control everything and everyone, but they must first learn to control themselves.

Crises teach "D's" humility. When they realize they are not as infallible and powerful as they thought, they can become broken. Out of brokenness, they can emerge with greater sensitivity and self-control. Crisis has a way of bringing us down to size. "D's" who turn "crisis" into "challenge" by controlling themselves can be the most powerful people in the world!

Chapter Twelve:

Practical Application for "I's"

"I's" are driven by their strong desires to impress and influence others. Try to find ways to recognize "I's" for their accomplishments, because approval is their most important motivating factor. Speak positively about them in public. Parents would be wise to telephone a friend or a relative, sharing how pleased they are about their "I" child's accomplishments. This praise should occur in front of the child, and the hearer's response should also present praise and reinforcement. Every child deserves this encouragement, but "I's" thrive on personal recognition.

The "I's" Have It

"I's" enjoy excitement — the more enthusiasm, the better. Some parents may really have to try to get excited, but it pays off for an "I" child. That is because "I's" long for group activities — they do not like playing alone. Involvement with lots of people motivates them — "the more the merrier!" They need frequent interaction with others.

Parents who cannot tolerate noise often avoid having their children's friends in their homes for any length of time. But parents of "I's" should work with their child's need for group interaction. For instance, it is possible to help children find ways of playing without so much noise and confusion. Find an exciting video program or encourage them to perform a play. Pretend that you are a movie agent who has heard how talented the group is. Ask them to write, direct and act out their own show for you. If you own a video camera, tape their performance, then watch it together. That should keep them busy for awhile. And it will also give your "I's" an opportunity to inspire and impress.

Understand that "I" children may easily get over-excited. They tend to be "too enthusiastic," which is why many parents of "I's" avoid group activities. Enthusiasm is good, but too much enthusiasm can lead to uncontrolled emotionalism. However, their children need more socialization than others, and it is to their benefit to allow and encourage group participation. You may need to oversee the sharing aspect of activities for younger children. They are still learning how to interact with one another.

Group Activities

Enroll your "I" child in group programs with a trained teacher or instructor. Sometimes, this structured environment is better for both the parent and the child. High "I's" need all the good discipline and training they can get. Don't just drop off your child at these events. Make it a habit to bring along your camera or video recorder to any school event, and take lots of pictures. Your child will love it.

"I's" need to express themselves. Asking them to obey without allowing them to question or share their feelings can frustrate them. It is not that they are questioning your authority; they simply need to verbalize when they feel pressure. Given enough time, some "I's" will even talk themselves into doing what they have resisted. They not only talk *you* in circles... they talk *themselves* in circles!

Don't try to "outtalk" an "I." Wait patiently and listen until he is ready for your response. That may never happen — so ask him to let you say something when he's finished! ("I'd like to say something about that when you're finished...") He will probably interrupt you and take off on another long-winded discourse. Again, wait for awhile, and then remind him that you were not finished. This probably will happen several times. But each time, you are making a greater impact and building a stronger case for him to improve his listening skills. "I's" are great talkers, but unfortunately they are poor listeners. They desperately need help in this area.

They Talk Too Much

Once talkative "I's" realize how patient you have been — and how rude they have been — you will have enough time to share your thoughts. They may not listen well, but it will make them think. This process helps them to better understand what you are trying to communicate.

It is usually a good idea to ask "I's" to share what they think you have just said to them. Do not condemn or attack them for not listening if they get it wrong. Simply question yourself for possibly not making your words clear enough, and then rephrase your statement. Good communication works both ways.

Give them another chance to explain what you are saying, until you both agree about the conversation. "I's" are good communicators when it comes to *talking,* but usually do poorly when it comes to *hearing* what is said.

"I's" need to learn how to "share the limelight." They are usually talented and love to show off. They tend to develop pride because of their intense desire for others to notice and praise them. Encourage them to overcome this tendency by complimenting their ability to handle losing graciously, or by explaining how impressed you are when they are willing to play second fiddle. Tell them you understand that it takes a "big person" to share with others the credit that they may deserve alone.

Disciplined Feelings

"I's" need to learn how to sit still and study, because preparation and planning are skills they generally do not possess. "I's" have the potential for making great grades, but they sometimes fail because they socialize too much. They do not attend school to learn very much. They go to see their friends! They do not like to miss any of the action... anywhere!

Parents can use their "I" children's desire to impress others as an encouragement to better grades. Use *rewards* that improve their self-image — perhaps new clothing or their own telephone may be appropriate at a certain age. Likewise, use *discipline* that motivates "I's" — to encourage study habits, perhaps no telephone privileges until they have finished their homework. Since they love to talk, there is a built-in reward for completing their task. Again, let them participate in their own disciplinary rules as you give "guidance" in the process. They will be surprisingly hard on themselves. Ask questions, rather than making dogmatic statements, and help them in the rule-making/decision-making process.

Suggest that your "I" child study with a friend — preferably a "C" who will encourage the "I" to be more thorough in his work. Use video or cassette teaching resources to help maintain your "I's" attention span. Excellent educational videos are available on virtually every topic through your local public library. My wife is constantly checking them out for the children/teens to watch. Since television is a prime teacher, why not use it for something good?

Find ways to relieve "I" children from sitting still for long periods of time. Get them to study for shorter intervals; ten or fifteen minutes at a time may be their natural, undisciplined limit. Encourage them to tell you what they have learned — or better yet, to demonstrate it. They love to show off, so challenge them to put their lessons and ideas to music, or even "rap." This may test your own limits as a parent, but it could be that your efforts will provide the motivation your "I" child needs to succeed.

"I's" are always motivated by *fun* ways of learning. One of my former students told me how she learned the eight parts of speech by singing the following song to the tune of "Turkey in the Straw":

> A noun's the name of anything
> > As a *house,* or *garden, boat* or *swing.*
> Instead of nouns you may prefer
> > The pronouns *you,* or *I,* or *her.*

> Adjectives tell the kind of noun
> > As *great, small, pretty, white* or *brown.*
> Verbs tell something to be done
> > As to *read, count, sing,* or *laugh* or *run.*

How things are done the adverbs tell
　As *slowly, quickly, ill* or *well.*
Conjunctions join two words together
　As men *and* women *or* wind *and* weather.

A preposition stands before a noun
　As *in* or *through* or *under* or *around.*
An interjection shows surprise —
　As *Oh!* how pretty, or *Ah!* how wise.

The whole are called eight parts of speech,
The whole are called eight parts of speech,
The whole are called eight parts of speech,
Which reading, writing, and speaking teach.

Don't you wish you had been taught this song as a child? Think how valuable it would have been in grammar class! Where was all the fun learning when we were growing up? It all depended on the teacher, didn't it? (Hint, hint!)

We have used the word "enthusiastic" to describe an "I" child. It may encourage parents of such children to understand the origin of this adjective. It is a combination of two Greek words: *en* + *theos* (*en* meaning "in" and *theos* meaning "God.)" Translated literally, it means God is inside and bubbling out! While you may think it is more likely that the devil is kicking up his heels than God is overflowing in your progeny, *this* is the way God has constructed *this* particular child. And He can gift you with grace and knowledge and wisdom and power and understanding to train up this child according to his own unique personality. This is what the Bible actually means when it refers to training a child "in the way he shall go."

Chapter Thirteen:

Practical Application for "S's"

"S's" respond best to kind words and gentle behavior. You should avoid raising your voice or losing your temper with "S's." They need security in easygoing environments.

"S's" back away from unstable situations and unsettling challenges. They are not risk-takers, and do not enjoy aggressive people. Avoid putting "S's" on the spot whenever possible.

"S's" do not become excited easily. They may even seem disinterested or bored, but it is their nature to *appear* so. "S's" are likely to become your best friends because of their undying loyalty. They want to stand by you and help you in any way they can.

Time to Recover

Give "S's" time to adjust. They prefer slow and gradual change, and they need time to respond without being pushed. They don't like surprises. If you know there is going to be a change involving an "S," warn him far enough in advance that he can prepare for it. An "S" word that they do not like is **surprise**! While it's not in his nature to resist or rebel, he will be less than enthusiastic if not given enough space and time to adapt to change.

"High-touch" is important to "S's." They want to feel like a part of the family. Greeting them with an appropriate hug or grasping their hand with both of yours is welcomed. Everyone has a need for intimacy, but "S's" respond the best to a warm and sincere touch.

Just Say "No!"

One of the most important things "S's" need to learn is how to say "No!" Although extremely difficult, it is possible. They tend to be **suckers**, agreeing to anything anyone asks them to do. They are vulnerable and can easily have advantage taken of them.

Assertiveness training is a practical help. As difficult as they may find it, "S's" can stand firm. Their love for people and their extreme loyalty make them easy prey for opportunistic, unscrupulous individuals. Volunteering as "a way of life" must be limited and controlled by the "S."

"S's" should not feel guilty for saying "No," nor worry that they may have hurt people or let the group down. Someone else can do the task when they need to decline.

Don't Work Harder — Think Smarter

"S's" need to learn how to turn a request for help into a

"challenging opportunity" for others. "S's" with unusually assertive attitudes can be a powerful stimulus to groups that constantly depend on them to get the job done.

Rather than being "reliable rescuers" or "emotional enablers," "S's" can learn to be *bold enough* to challenge "D's" to volunteer. They can learn to be *enthusiastic enough* to stimulate "I's" to participate. They can learn to be *convincing enough* to get "C's" to respond. Leadership, for an "S," is a most difficult task — but it can be their most powerful example!

"S's" cringe at the thought of being pioneers. They fit better into the mold of **settlers**. Therefore, they should become involved in projects that enlarge the borders of their self-imposed limits and protective *comfort zones*. Learning how to adapt and respond to new stresses can be helpful.

The Incredible Turtle

"S's" have the potential to turn into turtles! By retreating into their shells, "S's" protect themselves from the possible danger of being bruised and bumped.

Taking a public speaking course is the ultimate challenge for an "S." The thought of getting up in front of people and speaking is terrifying to them, but the discipline can result in tremendous growth.

Most of the "S's" problems stem from letting other people run over them. Reading books and listening to cassette tapes about self-worth and positive thinking can be beneficial for them. Zig Ziglar is one of the best teachers on that subject. You can find his resources in almost any bookstore.

Self-help can be beneficial for every personality, but obsession with self is dangerous and unhealthy. Knowing this, you can gently rest in the understanding that God *does* want us to feel good about ourselves. It was Ethel Waters who coined the phrase, "God don't make no junk!" We are fearfully and wonderfully made in the image of God. We have potential to improve and grow into something marvelous. Like a caterpillar in its cocoon, God can make us into the beautiful butterfly He created us to be.

Worm Theology

The problem with many people is that they equate their caterpillar status with that of a worm. We need to focus on what we can become and stretch our wings. We need to expand our emotions and actions beyond our personal *comfort zones* if we will learn to fly. (We understand that the effort of spinning its sheltering cocoon and then breaking free of its restraints is *the* struggle of a butterfly's life! No one said our struggles would be easy... just worth it!)

One Step At A Time

Fear cripples "S's." They often refuse to try new things or take advantage of new opportunities simply because they are afraid of the unknown. The heart of the problem lies *within* their hearts: fear. Though fear can, at times, be healthy, it can be equally stifling. "S's" need to rise above those emotions, to experience the challenge and satisfaction of venturing into the unknown.

Instead of refusing a challenge completely, "S's" can attempt small steps toward accepting new responsibilities. In this way, they can discover how easily new victories can be won. They should not be pushed into big challenges, but can be shown how little things can make a difference. "Inch by inch anything's a cinch — but by the yard, it's hard!"

Fear of failure, coupled with fear of the unknown, is more than most "S's" want to tackle. It would be helpful for them to redefine F–E–A–R as **F**alse **E**vidence **A**ppearing **R**eal! By eliminating their mountain of fear and replacing it with rolling hills of determination, "S's" can deal with anything!

Chapter Fourteen:

Practical Application for "C's"

The best advice for "C's" is to settle occasionally for less than perfection. Their constant inquiries can be nerve-racking; their need for answers can cause stress in relationships.

Recognizing a "C's" need to fully understand will help others to cope with their incessant inquisitiveness. Try the reverse "why?" response with them — "Why do you ask why?" It will force them to think through their question and perhaps answer it for themselves.

"Know–It–Alls"

"C's" usually are not being disrespectful when they repeatedly question things; they just want explanations. Their drive to comprehend and challenge the limits causes them sometimes to appear rebellious. Actually, they just want to go by the book. When they don't understand, they can become difficult.

Stimulate them to think through situations on their own,

and encourage them to use initiative to demonstrate competence. Reason goes a long way with "C's." The problem is, your explanation will probably create more questions for them to ask. So, patience is a great virtue for you to exhibit when dealing with "C's."

"C's" tend to be more task-oriented than most people. Feelings are not as important to them, so they may say or do things that seem cold and uncaring. Don't try to appeal to their emotions — appeal to a "C's" reasoning mind.

Recognize that they tend to be moody when they are in deep thought. They usually are not angry or upset; they just *act* like it! Give them some room to possibly misunderstand you or question you. Understand that their confusion often is expressed as displeasure.

Stinging Words

"C's" can be very caustic. However, they prefer to avoid conflict whenever possible. Under pressure, they shoot straight and take no prisoners. They attack when pushed, using the facts at hand. They say what they think and think about what they say. Often, they are right on target.

The "C" characteristic of "telling it like it is" often gets them into trouble. Most people don't like to hear the truth. "C's" need to learn how to "speak the truth in love." They must learn to season their speech with sensitivity — otherwise, they will take what appears obvious to them and beat you over the head with it — until it is blatant and you are bloody!

Because "C's" tend to worry more than others, it is important that they be surrounded with people who tend to be more optimistic. (A "C" and an "I" can really make a great pair if they *want to expend the effort* it takes to work together.) And don't be surprised when a "C" shows impatience with those who want to help. They have a knack for finding fault with others assisting them. They feel they can do things quite well by themselves. Although they may not enjoy it initially, optimism is good for "C's." They are naturally pessimistic, so keeping them happy is difficult.

Thorns In The Flesh

"C's" are "rally killers" and "party poopers." They really have a difficult time doing "The Wave" at a baseball game! They dump cold water on a hot idea faster than anyone else. But what they say is often very insightful. It is important to listen to "C's" advice without writing them off because of their negativism.

Be careful not to miss a "C's" wisdom because you dislike his attitude. Your responses to his concerns and cautions will either encourage or discourage him to open up. Too often, a "C" will sit and stew, contributing nothing, because once they were criticized for something they did or said.

"C's" try to — and need to — be more positive. They should imagine seeing life through rose-colored glasses; they should smell the roses and see the bright side of things. Occasionally, "C's" should search for the pot of gold at the end of the rainbow, rather than glaring at the rain clouds and puddles that accompany such weather conditions. They should whistle and sing and smile more — and see how much better life can be. Remember Bobby McFerrin's Emmy Award-winning song, "Don't Worry, Be Happy"? "C's" would do well to hum that tune to themselves throughout the day.

Just As I Thought

I can imagine "C's" thinking as they read this material, "How corny — how absolutely ridiculous!" But that is exactly what I mean — their initial response is usually negative. "C's" can take these insights to heart, improving the quality of their lives and the lives of those who are tired of their "gloom, despair, and agony on me" attitudes. The challenge most "C's" face is that they are usually right! But people don't want friends who are *always* right — they want friends who will forgive and forget, who pick each other up rather than picking each other apart.

Incompetent People Skills

"C's" can develop their social skills by becoming involved in social activities, or by taking up hobbies that involve others. Finding an activity that forces the "C" to relate and to express his feelings helps him become more sensitive to those around him.

Above all, "C's" should manage their natural tendency toward depression by learning to control their feelings of inadequacy and incompetence. We live in an imperfect world with imperfect people — relax! Learn how to enjoy life. You don't always have to understand or explain everything.

"C's" tend to be the most competent people in the world. Learn how they think and feel, and you will be able to work better with them. If you are a "C," learn to appreciate the thinking and feeling processes of others. You will gain credibility when you concentrate on "winning the right to be heard" rather than concentrating on sharing critical views and harsh judgments.

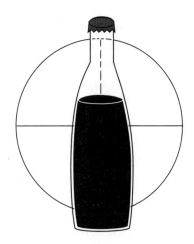

Chapter Fifteen:

Adapting and Adjusting

Dealing with another person according to his personality type is like trying to speak another language. If you know how to speak someone's native tongue, you will be able to communicate well. If not, you will be frustrated at best, and at worst you will get nowhere at all!

Not long ago, some friends of mine were checking into a hotel in San Antonio, Texas. A young, Hispanic bellman loaded their suitcases on his cart and started rolling them down the hall toward their rooms. Tom, realizing that he needed some traveler's checks, said to him, "Wait a minute... I need something from one of those bags." The bellman never slowed down nor turned around. Tom said, a little louder, "Wait a minute — I need my bag." The bellman kept going. Finally, Tom yelled at him, "Wait a minute!" Still, the bellman never broke stride. Another friend in the group said to Tom, "I don't think yelling louder is going to help him understand English."

You guessed it — the bellman spoke only Spanish. In

order to communicate with him, Tom needed to speak his language. How softly or loudly Tom spoke had nothing to do with communicating. The secret was speaking in a way that allowed him to understand and respond.

In a similar manner, we must learn to speak in ways that communicate clearly with people of different personality types. Communication is not merely the process of you speaking some words in *your* language. To really communicate, you must learn to speak in a way your listener can understand. Believe it or not, this isn't difficult or impossible. It just takes a little time and effort — like learning any new language requires. However, after you begin to practice the four key points of view (that dominate the four personality styles discussed in Chapter 6), you will be able to communicate more effectively, and your interactions will become "win–win" situations. You will try to communicate to others *in their language,* and they in turn will understand you!

Providing A Safe Environment

As the Golden Gate Bridge was being built, 23 people fell to their deaths. Because of its incredible height, workers feared falling. Eventually the project slowed to a "snail's pace." Something had to be done. A huge net was installed, at an unanticipated additional cost of $100,000. Some viewed it as an entirely unnecessary expense, but what happened? Almost overnight, work picked up. Morale was back, and men worked faster than ever. Several fell from their perches but to no harm — they were caught by the net. Not only was the project completed on time, but no other lives were lost in the process.

In a similar manner, care should be taken in understanding your family, friends and co-workers. If you take the time to learn about their "safety nets" — their internal, basic thought processes and needs — then building relationships will "speed up" and you will make greater progress with fewer casualties. Here are four additional keys to remember when trying to communicate with any personality type:

1. *Voice Tones*

People are a lot like dogs in the sense that they hear our voice tones even more than they hear our words. It cannot be overemphasized how important voice tones are. Research indicates that the majority of what is communicated in a message is not in our actual words but in the quality and volume of our voice tones.

Try this experiment at home. Stomp your foot at your dog and yell, "You're a good dog and I like you!" If your dog is normal, he will lower his head, put his tail between his legs and shy away from you. Look at him and say in a happy, sweet tone, "You're a bad dog and you stink!" His tail will begin to wag, and he will want to jump into your arms. Obviously, he doesn't understand what you say, but he hears the way you say it.

Both "I's" and "S's" are much more susceptible to tones than to words. It is important for them to *feel* love, rather than *hear* it, because they are so people-oriented. "D's" and "C's" are prone to interpret your words by your voice tones, too. And they react negatively when they sense an antagonistic environment. Vocal nuances play a vital role in all your relationships. We will do well to remember how important our voice tones really are.

2. *Timing*

When dealing with any of the personality types, timing is very important. If we are going to help people or influence them for good, we must do so in a nonthreatening manner. Confronting someone about his behavior when he is dominated by his personality influences (and out of control) will probably do no good. To tell a high "I" that he has been talking nonstop, without letting anyone else get in a word, will only cause him to feel hurt — and not to like you because you are obviously not a nice person. It is more productive to wait until a neutral time and a private place to share this personality insight material with him and keep him as a friend.

Think of it this way: Most people try to help an alcoholic at the worst possible time; namely, when he is drunk! But a drunk person will only get mad at you and may even try to hurt you if you intrude. It is a far better idea to approach him over a nice meal and talk intelligently, openly and honestly with him when he is sober. It is the strategy that yields better results.

Here is an illustration from nature: Suppose you went into an orchard and picked an apple from a tree. The tree and the apple are sturdy and rugged — apples can be picked without causing damage. But what if on your way from the orchard you saw a rose bush in full bloom and decided to pick a few roses? What if you grabbed the blossom and pulled on it just as you did the apple? It would fall apart in your hand. You can't pick roses the same way you pick apples! Profound!

The distinction lies not just within apples and roses, but within each of us. *We* must treat apples and roses differently because they *are* different. And we must treat people differently for the same reason. If we can begin to consciously practice adjusting our presentation style to meet the need of the moment, we will be better off and more productive in our relationships.

3. *Recognizing Control Versus Change*

One question I am commonly asked as I teach personality seminars across the country is, "Can we change our personalities?" Let me respond with several thoughts.

First, the primary issue should not be *change*. I firmly believe the emphasis should be on *control*. Can I control my personality? Can I, as a "D," at one time be dominant and in control of a certain set of circumstances? Can I, as a "D," also be submissive and help you in your situation? As an "I," can I be inspirational and talk? And can I also be quiet and listen to you talk? As an "S," can I at one opportunity help in your need? And can I also be assertive and say, "I would like to be in charge of that project!"? Can I, as a "C," be cautious and want everything done correctly — but on the other hand still step out on faith to take an occasional risk?

We will always be most comfortable where our genes and environment have led us thus far in life. However, if you want to *adjust* — a more accurate term than "change" — you can certainly do so.

If a right-handed person loses his ability to use that hand, he can learn to write with his left. He may not *feel* as comfortable as he once did, but he can *adapt* and *adjust* with excellent results. We can all learn to adapt if we desire strongly to do so. It will always be *easier* for us to function in our most comfortable mode; however, it may not be to our *good* or *interest* to do so.

By understanding all four personality types, we can adjust ourselves to be more efficient and effective in any situation. For instance, if a high "D" type joins the United States Marine Corps, he will learn that it is best to "be more 'S'" and do as he is told. However, when he is discharged, his "D" type personality will "kick back in." Hopefully, through discipline and maturity, he will have learned the benefits of controlling his personality drives over attempting to change his personality. Change is a wonderful by-product or result of self-control, but I don't believe change should be the focus.

I have a friend who also has four daughters. He told me the difficulty he had in being spontaneously affectionate with them because "all that touching and hugging and kissing" was just not the way he was raised. Although my friend loves God, has gone through therapy, and deeply loves his children, I doubt that his "feeler" will ever change. I told him not to worry about how he "felt." Just recognize the challenge, then *control* himself to reach out tenderly and lovingly to his girls, rather than wait until he feels he can *change*. Find *control* first, then *change* will follow.

4. *Understand How to See the Real Person*

This bottle illustration is an "object lesson" showing how we typically observe and evaluate people. We often go by what we see on the surface. In the diagram, the top portion of the bottle represents the "surface" personality, and it is labeled "polite, informal, cordial, cultural." By this I mean that most people (regardless of their personality type) function on the "polite, informal, cordial, cultural" level when they first meet someone. Let's face it, we all want to make a good first impression, and we know we relate best to others — especially those with whom we are not closely acquainted — when we employ a cordial, polite demeanor. So, this informal behavior of our more outgoing, people-oriented "better self" may be observed much of the time, when we are having a meal, enjoying a sports event, or functioning on a "surface level" with others.

But this is not the "substance" of the bottle — it is only at the "air" at the top. The actual personality is revealed "when the top is popped" and relationships begin to develop. As we become more intimate or familiar, our true personality will be revealed. The real content of the bottle is beneath its surface.

I suppose we could really carry the analogy to extremes by pointing out that a soft drink bottle's "fizz" or lack thereof is like one personality type or another... Or that the way a soft drink bottle foams when you shake it resembles what happens when someone with a certain personality type gets shaken up... Or that some people are "caffeine free" in their personalities while others really "wake things up..." Or that one personality is genuinely sweet, while another uses artificial sweetness... Or that one personality style is more like the "uncola," while another is more like "the real thing..." But my real point is that what we first observe on the surface is not a reliable clue to the real content of people's personalities.

I jokingly say in my seminars that dating is one of the most deceitful times in human experience. We expose to the person we are dating our polite, cordial, informal, cultural nature — as though it is the "real us." In reality, we are covering up many of our weaknesses, in order to "put our best foot forward." Eventually, after "capturing" the mate we have pursued, our guard drops and our "real" personality is revealed. That is why husbands and wives often say, "You are not the person I married!" It *is* the person you married... you just didn't know that person well enough.

When I give the Personality Profile to couples I counsel, it reveals their real personalities to themselves and to each other. In premarital counseling, I share what each person's real tendencies are, to give the couple a view of reality. After a couple is already married, I explain to them that since it is true that opposites *attract,* then sooner or later they will begin to *attack!*

We must learn to see life beyond our own limited perspective and learn to see it from our mate's viewpoint as well. If you were standing back-to-back with your mate, you know both of you would have a different view. Each would see things the other could not see. It is to our advantage to listen as our partner explains what he or she is seeing. This viewpoint will help us to understand and complement other views that cannot be seen or appreciated clearly through the limited lens of our own personality.

When people first meet or are dating, they go out of their way to be nice to each other. Manners, customs and culture dictate that necessity — unless, of course, you don't care if people are repelled by you! But after they have worked together on a daily basis, or have traveled together for an extended time, or have plighted their troth to each other, then they begin to meet the *real* people involved in the relationship.

At this point, one decides whether or not to continue exercising control and displaying the attractive characteristics of their polite, informal, cordial, cultural personality. Doing so maintains good relationships. Losing control of the personality offends people. We each make that choice, whether we *know* it or not... and whether we *like* it or not!

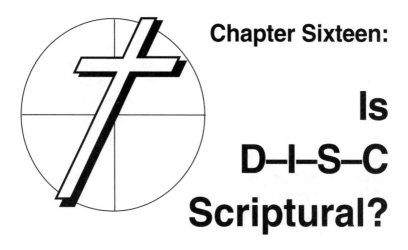

Chapter Sixteen:

Is
D–I–S–C
Scriptural?

I am often asked, "If this personality information is so important, why isn't it in the Bible?" I always respond in two ways:

First, *all truth* belongs to God — everything in the Bible is true. However, there is a lot of "additional truth" God chose not to include in the Bible, like the multiplication tables, the Periodic Table of Elements, penicillin, etc. God fully expects that we will learn many things apart from the Bible. The Book of Romans explains that we can learn much truth from observing the natural world (Romans 1:20). It is vital that we examine "additional truth" in the light of God's Word, rather than attempting to examine God's Word in the light of new "revelation." But we can't shun knowledge — let's face it, we even had to possess the knowledge of how to read before we could read the Bible!

Part of the hesitancy many Christians feel in approaching temperaments or other explanations of the human condition is their fear that unbiblical theories will supplant Scripture. Some teaching on the "Four Temperament" Model of Human Behavior has left some people feeling they have an excuse for their own out-of-control behavior, rather than empowering them for controlled behavior. In effect, it becomes "astrology for Christians" when believers say, "Oh well, I'm a sanguine... I'm a high 'I'... and that's just the way I operate!" Or, "It's my personality style to be negative — learn to accept me as I am." Or, "If God really loves me, He wouldn't have given me such a dumb personality profile. Now I'm stuck with what I don't like." (There's no significant difference between those "personality excuses" and a person who doesn't even believe God exists and says, "I'm an Aries, so this is my fate.")

The Bible tells us to "take every thought captive to the obedience of Christ." That simply means we must examine all of life in a way that keeps us in harmony with God's wisdom and truth. When we are exhorted to "have the *mind* of Christ," it means God wants our hearts and personalities and actions to be conformed to His: well-balanced and responsive. We do this best by understanding our strengths and weaknesses.

Secondly, I believe D–I–S–C insights are found in many places in Scripture, only not labeled as such. "Well," you might ask, "was Jesus a 'D,' or an 'I,' or an 'S,' or a 'C'?" In answer to that question, I say emphatically, "Yes!" The life of Christ reveals all the positive traits of each personality type. He was a perfect balance of all four types. Controlled by the Holy Spirit and surrendered to His Father's purposes, I believe Jesus displayed the truly integrated and complete personality which God purposed for mankind. We marvel at His humanity, unmarred by sin. When we compare our fragmented personalities to His, we can see the distortion of God's image that a fallen "human nature" has brought about in our own lives.

In Chapters 2–5, we cited examples of New Testament characters who displayed specific personality types. In addition to those examples, in I Corinthians 9:19–23, the Apostle Paul makes an interesting point concerning human personalities: "To the strong, I have become strong; to the weak, I have become weak. I have become all things to all men that I might by all means win some and I do this for the sake of the gospel." You can't adapt yourself to another's personality unless you first understand personality styles! It is easy to win people to Jesus after you first win them to *yourself.* Paul said, in effect, "I know how to build rapport. I make myself a specialist in understanding other people." That's the purpose of our study together, to gain a better understanding of ourselves and others, to build better relationships.

How did Jesus use this model of human behavior? Here are several examples:

When He went into the Temple, He overturned the tables and threw out the money changers. Was that the "normal personality" of Jesus? I think not. While all four Gospels tell the story, only John reveals that He "sat down and braided a whip" before going back into the Temple court (John 2:14–17). Did He have a "Tandy Whip Maker's Kit" with Him at the time? No, He got the materials he needed, and then He sat down and put the whip together. What an example of strength under control! His driving out the money changers was not an emotional outburst — He wasn't out of control. Rather, He "raised his 'D'" type personality that day, because **demanding, dramatic, driving, dynamic** "D" type action was required. With the whip and a voice of command He said, "Out! This is My Father's house. This is a house of prayer, and you have turned it into a den of thieves! Get out!"

Have you ever wondered why temple guards didn't just grab Jesus and make Him stop what He was doing? Think about this: Jesus was a carpenter — do you know where carpenters got the wood with which they worked? They cut down their own trees in the woods. Our image of Jesus as a mild, meek, wimpy-looking person is a misconception. He grew up with an axe in His hands! Muhammad Ali once trained for a heavyweight boxing championship fight by cutting down trees... and he knocked out his opponent in the first round! He said later, "I'll never train that way again. I was over-ready for that fight. Cutting down trees is the hardest thing I've ever done!"

I imagine on that particular day in the temple someone said, "Grab that man and make him stop!" And someone else probably said, "If he's bothering you, why don't *you* grab him?" I believe Jesus was a man's man, and that day when He said, "Everybody out!", they got out!

Again, this wasn't His standard method of dealing with people or with problems. However the Bible reveals on a few occasions that He was capable of "raising his 'D'" when issues required a bold, firm stand.

On another occasion, Jesus raised His "I" profile. Can you see Him in front of 4,000 men, plus women and children (Matthew 15:29–39)? He loved the crowds enthusiastically most of the time, and was sensitive to their needs. He had spent three days with them, being **inspirational**, **influencing**, **interactive** and **interesting**. "These people are hungry... let's eat. What is available?" All His disciples could scrounge up were seven loaves of bread and a few small, smoked fish. Jesus' thought was, "What we need to do now is eat. Have everybody sit down. I'm going to treat!" Typically, high "I's" do this without even thinking: let's talk... let's eat! Jesus knew when His **inspirational**, **influencing**, **interactive**, **interesting** personality style was effective.

As a friend read this section in manuscript form, she commented, "All the high 'I's' I have ever met are so flamboyant in front of a crowd — I just can't imagine Jesus being out of control as an 'I'." What great insight! His behavior in this setting demonstrates a *controlled* "I." To exhibit these traits in balance demonstrates a Spirit-controlled personality.

Jesus "raised his 'S'" when He washed His disciples' feet, and again when He welcomed the little children. The disciples had pushed them aside to make room for more important adults. They didn't want the Master troubled by dirty little faces and incessant small talk. He said, "Let the children alone, and do not hinder them from coming to Me; for the kingdom of heaven belongs to such as these" (Matthew 19:13–15).

Little children can read adults very well. Would they have wanted to be with Jesus if they perceived that He was an out-of-control "D" or "I"? Would they have warmed to Him as a cautious "C"? What drew them was His **steady**, **stable**, **secure**, **servant** heart. He took them in His arms and blessed them. He knew how to conform His personality to the situation, so children could feel that He was approachable — and they came to sit on His lap.

Jesus exercised his high "C" profile on another occasion. I love the insight in this story! Scribes and Pharisees asked Him, "Where do you get your authority to do these things?" High "C's" love questions. So, Jesus turned the tables on them: "Before I answer, let me ask you a question. Where did John (the Baptist) get his authority?" They said, "Just a minute..." Then they walked away from the crowd for a hasty huddle: "If we say John spoke as a man, the crowd will stone us to death because they believe he was a prophet. But if we say his authority came from God, Jesus will ask why we didn't believe him." So they came back to Jesus and said, "We cannot answer that question." And Jesus replied, "Then I can't answer the question you have asked me." And the Bible says, "...from that day forward, no one asked Him any more questions" (Luke 20:1–40).

Jesus displayed his **competent**, **conscientious**, **correct**, **critical** thinking, **convinced**, **consistent** skills in dealing with these **cautious**, **calculating**, **controlling conformists**. You see, Jesus knew how to deal with people: "Eye for an eye, tooth for a tooth... 'C' for a 'C'!"

My favorite demonstration of how Jesus "adjusted" His personality is found in John 11:14–35. His friend, Lazarus, had died. Jesus went to see the family. Martha came to Him and said, "Master, if you had been here, my brother would not have died." He replied, "Martha, your brother will live again!" She said, "I know he will live again at the resurrection on the last day." Jesus said, "I am the Resurrection. He who believes in me, though he were dead, yet shall he live. Do you believe this, Martha?" She responded, "I believe that you are the Messiah, the Son of God." Martha came to Jesus with all these questions... and Jesus provided "quality answers."

Several verses later, we see that the other sister, Mary, also came to Jesus. She said, "Lord, if you had been here, my brother would not have died." She spoke exactly the same words

Martha had spoken previously. But in response, Scripture says, "Jesus wept."

"Wait a minute, Lord," we could say, "I don't understand! Martha comes up to you and you give her explanations. Mary says the same thing, and you begin weeping. Why?" I was praying about this and it was like a light came on in my spirit! Martha came to Jesus with a broken *mind*, so He gave her an *explanation* with quality answers. Mary came to Jesus with a broken *heart*, so He responded with *tears*. Fantastic! Jesus adjusted His treatment because He knew they had very different *needs*. And if you look at the other references to Lazarus' two sisters, you will see they also had very different personalities. (See John 12:1–7 and Luke 10:38–42.) If we can adjust the way we approach and relate to people, it will make all the difference in the world!

Romans 15:2 states, "Each of us should please his neighbor for his good, to build him up." How can we practice this truth without understanding personality insights? I trust you are now better equipped to apply this command as a result of reading this book. If so, you will have helped me to obey this command in writing it, as well. That's what I call a "win–win" situation. This is what I have directed my efforts toward. Thanks for reading. I hope our time together has been helpful. God bless you!

Appendix A

A Child's Uniqueness

The Hebrew text of Proverbs 22:6 *(ha NOK la NA ar al pi dar KO)* literally reads: "Train [start] a child according to his [the child's] way." There is a great difference between the training of a child according to the *child's* way (i.e., encouraging him to start on the road that is right for him) and training him according to a way chosen, prescribed and imposed by the parents. The former is in keeping with the child's special, God-given bent, disposition, talents and gifts. It is considerate of the uniqueness of the child; it does not treat all developing personalities the same.

This translation and interpretation put the onus on the *child* to choose the right path. It is one thing for a parent to encourage, nurture, guide and inform, so that the child *himself* is prepared to choose the path that is right for him; it is something else for a parent to choose the child's path. This point is the crux to understanding this verse.

Again, we must emphasize that this rendering does not

negate the parents' role as teachers of biblical truth and tradition. But it does provide some additional insight into the Hebrew educational process which, parenthetically, corresponds well with certain modern schools of progressive education.

This "training" process begins by seeking to conform the subject matter and teaching methods to the particular personality, needs, grade level and stage in the life of the child. It does not suggest conforming the child to the demands of an inflexible curriculum. (The word *NA ar*, "child," in Proverbs 22:6 does not necessarily mean "infant" or "small boy"; its more than 200 occurrences in Scripture reveal a wide range of meanings, from childhood to maturity.) Thus, the ability of a "child" to exercise more and more of his individual freedom by personal choice — albeit one *informed* by his parents — is certainly not ruled out.

A Tall Order

By way of application, this understanding of Proverbs 22:6 places a special responsibility upon every parent. Parents must closely observe each child and seek to provide opportunities for each child's creative self-fulfillment. In addition, parents must be sensitive to the direction in life to which the child would naturally conform — for it is only by walking in that path that the child will come to realize his God-given potential and find his highest fulfillment.

Elizabeth O'Connor effectively grasps how this Proverb may apply:
"Every child's life gives forth hints and signs of the way he is to go. The parent who knows how to mediate stores these hints and signs away and ponders over

them. We are to treasure the intimations of the future that the life of every child gives to us so that, instead of unconsciously putting blocks in his way, we help him to fulfill his destiny. This is not an easy way to follow. Instead of telling our children what they should do and become, we must be humble before their wisdom, believing that in them, and not in us, is the secret they need to discover." (O'Connor, Elizabeth. *Eighth Day of Creation,* Waco, TX: Word Books, 1971, p. 18.)

This is a tall order. But when parents see that their responsibility is primarily to facilitate, to teach the child to choose the right path, only then will the child be able to "fulfill his destiny." And herein lies an important educational key to making learning a sweet and palatable adventure.

> – Adapted from: *Our Father Abraham: Jewish Roots of the Christian Faith* (Grand Rapids, MI: Eerdmans Publishing Company; Center for Judaic–Christian Studies, 1989, pp. 291–294)

Appendix B

The "Four Behavior-Style" Theories

Models have been developed through the years in an attempt to understand, explain and predict human behavior. Hippocrates developed the "classic" or Medieval model based on his presumption that a balance of bodily fluids determines temperament. To account for a broader range of behaviors, psychiatry has defined some 13 distinct personality variations. Since our concern is understanding the general population with normal emotions, and not the seriously disturbed, the "Four Behavior-Style" theory is an excellent model. When it is explained properly, it can be applied easily.

The following examples generally conform to this overview (shown at the left) which indicates assertive behaviors and responsive attitudes.

High Assertiveness Low Responsiveness	High Assertiveness High Responsiveness
Low Assertiveness High Responsiveness	Low Assertiveness Low Responsiveness

Hippocrates not only missed the boat in his idea that phlegm *(flem)* made people behave as they do — he left us with difficult "name-tags" for these behaviors. ⇾

Choleric	Sanguine
Melancholy	Phlegmatic

Source: *"Medieval Four Temperaments"*

Power	Integration
Suppression	Denial

Source: *"Conflict-Styles: Organizational Decision Making"*
— Donald T. Simpson

◁— There is a hierarchy at work in the model to the left that seems to scream for corporate maneuvering and inkblot testing.

Word choices influence how easily these concepts can be remembered, and with each variation, new insights can be gained. ⇾

Driver	Expressive
Analytical	Amiable

Source: *"Personal Styles and Effective Performances"*
— David W. Merrill - Rodger H. Hill

Competing	Collaborating
Accommodating	Avoiding

Source: *"Conflict Mode Instrument"*
— Thomas - Kilmann

◁— The model at the left is alliterative and simple. Its scope is limited to cooperative skills and expectations in conflict resolution.

Our goal is a model that guides and informs us in a variety of experiences. The "labels" at the right indicate teamwork philosophies and even negotiating patterns.—▷

Win / Lose	Synergistic
Yield / Lose	Lose / Leave

Source: "Conflict Management Survey"
— Jay Hall

Controlling Taking	Adapting Dealing
Supporting Giving	Conserving Holding

Source: "Basic Systems"
— Stuart Atkins, Lifo (Life Orientations)

◁— On the left, we see an adjective that describes the personality's basic objective — and a verb that shows how the objective is reached.

This is similar to the "Outgoing vs. Reserved" and "Task- vs. People-Oriented" orientation which influences our temperament model. —▷

Dominant Hostile	Dominant Warm
Submissive Hostile	Submissive Warm

Source: "Effective Motivation Through Performance Appraisal" — Robert E. Lefton

D Dominant	**I** Influencing
C Cautious	**S** Supportive

Source: "Emotions of Normal People"
— William M. Marston

◁— The most easily understood teaching regarding personality styles is based on the "D-I-S-C" model, as taught by Marston, Geier and others.

How to Understand Yourself & Others video Dr. Rohm presents this three-hour Video Seminar with energy and excitement before a "live" studio audience of business owners. Audience involvement makes you feel like you're there! Three hours of fast-paced, fun instruction. (Produced in association with InterNET Services Corporation. 2-tape video album available in VHS format only.) Price $40.00

Break Through the Walls cassettes Dr. Rohm's three-hour Video Seminar (above) sound track on three quality audio cassettes! Includes an "Introduction to the Model of Human Behavior," the "D," "I," "S," and "C" types, and "Understanding Personality Blends." Great stories supplement the technical material. Now includes a pocket-size version of the Funbook so you can follow along. Listen while you drive, jog, work out, or rake the yard so your neighbors will like you (if you don't "get it," you haven't heard the seminar yet!). Price $20.00

Complete Seminar Kit This is like attending the complete "Understanding Yourself and Others" Seminar again and again. You receive two video tapes (above), six cassette tapes (the seminar soundtrack) for use in your car, plus four FUNBOOKS (which Dr. Rohm uses with the studio audience), one Case Studies booklet, and four Self-Scoring Questionnaires. Ideal for small groups. Additional supplies are available in our catalog. Price $89.00

Add 10% shipping ($3.00 minimum). Georgia residents add appropriate sales tax. Prices subject to change.

Please contact us to request our complete catalog.
PERSONALITY INSIGHTS, INC.
P.O. Box 28592 • Atlanta, GA 30358 USA • (800) 509-DISC
or see it all on the web at *http://www.personality-insights.com*

Who Do You Think You Are... Anyway? How your unique style *acts, reacts* and *interacts* with others. Lots of great stories and examples, along with graphs and charts for quick and easy reference. Clear explanations of preferences, work habits and beneficial traits for all 29 possible blends — with detailed chapters showing you how to "DISCover" your spouse's and child's design, as well as your work design. (Appx. 350 pp.)
Price $14.95

Different Children, Different Needs Dr. Rohm collaborated on this book with Charles F. Boyd and David Boehi. Its theme is "the Art of Adjustable Parenting and Teaching," demonstrating how to discover each child's motivations and how to tailor your parenting style to meet each child's needs, using the D-I-S-C system. Price $11.95

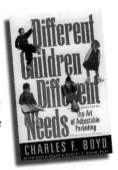

Tales Out of School As you read this *Revised Edition*, you'll discover why so many teachers say, "My students are my best teachers!" Real-life classroom events in short story form, seen through an understanding of personality styles. Compiled by Dr. Rohm from essays of school teachers and administrators who are using the DISC system in the classroom. Excellent for case studies and in-service training. (Appx. 300 pp.) Price $14.95

Self-scoring Style Assessment booklets contain the Questionnaire, Basic and Environmental charts and background information. Child and Teen profiles include a companion cassette tape. Price $10.00

Adult Profile

*(Note: You may order **additional** copies of any of these booklets without the cassette tape for $5.00)*

Teen Profile

Child Profile

About the Author

Dr. Robert A. Rohm is the president of Personality Insights, Inc., in Atlanta, GA. He has spoken to audiences in nearly every conceivable situation: schools, businesses, churches, weddings, funerals, children's groups, nursing homes, cruise ships, beaches, hospitals, college campuses, conventions, and others! He has traveled across America, Canada and Europe speaking, teaching and training people how to develop better relationships.

Dr. Rohm has served with Dr. Charles Stanley at First Baptist Church of Atlanta as Minister of Adult Education. Before moving to Atlanta, he was Associate Pastor of First Baptist Church, Dallas, TX, with Senior Pastor Dr. W. A. Criswell. He worked with Zig Ziglar's "Auditorium Class," and over 500 families in the church were under his care. In the field of education, he has been a classroom teacher, school administrator, and supervisor of curriculum development.

Dr. Rohm is a graduate of Dallas Theological Seminary, where he was named to the National Deans' List while earning his Th.M. degree. He received his Ph.D. in Higher Education Administration and Counseling from the University of North Texas. He is a recipient of the National Jaycees' "Outstanding Young Men in America" award, and has been listed in *Who's Who in the South and Southwest*. He is a member of the American Association of Christian Counselors.

Dr. Rohm is also a certified human behavior consultant, teaching parents specific ways to understand and motivate their children, and teaching adults ways to improve communication skills in marriage, work and dating relationships. He has been a keynote speaker at banquets, seminars and workshops across America. His unique blend of humor, stories and illustrations makes him a popular speaker with young and old alike.